healthy eating
for kids

over 100 meal ideas,
recipes and healthy eating
tips for children

anita bean

A&
CB

First published 2004 by
A & C Black Publishers Ltd
38 Soho Square, London W1D 3HB
www.acblack.com

Reprinted 2005

ISBN 07136 6917 9

A CIP catalogue record for this book is available from the British Library.

Note: Whilst every effort has been made to ensure that the content of this
book is as technically accurate and as sound as possible, neither the author nor
the publishers can accept responsibility for any injury or loss sustained as a
result of the use of this material.

Author photograph © Grant Pritchard
Kids' food images © BananaStock Ltd.
Food images © Comstock images
Food pyramid illustration on p.4 © Tina Howe

Typeset in Bembo by Fakenham Photosetting Limited, Norfolk

Printed and bound in Singapore by Tien Wah Press Pte.

A&C Black uses paper produced with elemental chlorine-free pulp, harvested
from managed sustainable forests.

contents

introduction

What this book is about: Eating for life

Unlike other books on kids' food, this one doesn't preach an evangelical diet, nor assume you have plenty of time to cook interesting meals. It's about feeding your child in the real world – healthily.

Here I've endeavoured to combine my expertise as a nutritionist, my knowledge as a health writer and my experience as a mother. It's one thing to know what children ought to eat, it's another making them eat it. Many a time has my patience been tested as my own children refuse vegetables, reject balanced meals, or pester me in the supermarket for foods they've seen advertised on the TV.

I also know how difficult it can be to say no when children insist on unhealthy snacks because their friends eat them, or when they'd rather nibble on chocolate than an orange. One thing is clear, what children eat now has a big impact on their health, fitness and – importantly – what they'll be eating in years to come. Establishing healthy eating habits today will give your children the best start in life.

To make it easier, try following these ten key steps:

■ teach by example – If they see you enjoying healthy meals, they're more likely to do the same.

■ keep to the 80/20 rule – if children eat a balanced diet around 80% of the time, then they're free to enjoy other foods they want the other 20% of the time.
■ be consistent – decide on your ground rules (what is and isn't allowed) and stick to them.
■ be persistent – children's tastes change and they will eventually learn to like what they're given.
■ involve them – include your children in menu planning, shopping and cooking as early as possible.
■ share mealtimes when you can and feed your children the same food you eat yourself.
■ make children feel valued – that way they'll be more likely to make healthier food and activity choices.
■ don't ban any food – it will only increase your child's desire for it – nor use food as a reward.
■ make meals as attractive, varied and imaginative as you can.
■ keep treat foods as treats and bring them into the house only on special occasions.

I hope that you'll find this book useful and inspirational.

anita

Acknowledgements

Thanks as ever to my husband, Simon, for keeping cool during lifes most hectic moments; and to my beautiful daughters, Chloe and Lucy, for giving me the opportunities to put everything in this book into practice – including surviving shopping with them, dealing with pester power, coercing them to eat their greens, devising healthy menus and recipes, cooking with them (and putting up with a very messy kitchen!) but, best of all, rewarding me with their enthusiasm for and love of healthy food.

I would also like to thank Linda Bird for her editorial expertise. Thanks to Charlotte Croft, Hannah McEwen and A&C Black for making this book possible.

Anita's daughters, Chloe and Lucy.

foreword

I was delighted when asked to write the foreword, not only because I know Anita, but because *Healthy Eating for Kids* is written with considerable expertise and I am sure it will go a long way to helping parents feed their children well.

One in ten children are obese – three times more than 10 years ago. It's important for our children and their children that we tackle the obesity problem because if we don't we shall be storing up major health problems. If present trends continue, at least a third of girls and a fifth of boys will be obese by 2020.

Children are eating too many snacks, fast foods and ready meals that are high in fat, sugar and salt. They are also spending more time in front of the TV or computer and not taking enough physical activity. Too many get driven to school and schools have reduced the actual time spent on PE.

A book about children's nutrition therefore needs to be both comprehensive and inspiring. It requires lots of practical ideas and strategies to help parents overcome the problems of feeding their children healthy foods.

Anita has successfully combined all of these ingredients resulting in a book that is accurate and exciting and written in an easy to follow style. Here, she brings together years of expertise as a nutritionist, as well as a mother who understands the challenges of feeding children. This book is packed with useful facts, clever tips, tasty recipes and inspiring ideas that will transform family meal times and your child's nutrition – for good.

Enjoy!

Paul Gately BA (Hons) MMedSci PhD
Principal Lecturer in Exercise Physiology and Health
Director of the Carnegie International Children's Weight Loss Camp
Leeds Metropolitan University

what should your children eat?

What children eat affects their health both now and in the future. They need a balanced diet to grow properly, keep healthy and fight off illnesses. A nutritious diet means your children will:

- have plenty of energy
- feel bright and alert
- concentrate better at school
- suffer fewer illnesses
- have clear skin, bright eyes and shiny hair.

The earlier you teach children healthy eating and exercise habits, the better. A healthy diet now means a healthy diet in ten years' time. Children don't 'grow out of' poor eating habits – they continue eating the foods they're used to being given.

It's not always easy to persuade children to make healthy choices but try to stick to the 80/20 rule. This means eating a balanced diet around 80% of the time, while the other 20% of the time, children are free to enjoy other foods they want.

What is a balanced diet?

Eating a balanced diet is all about eating a wide variety of foods. Your children's diet should provide them with all the vital nutrients needed to keep them fit and well. A healthy diet consists of a balance of protein, carbohydrate, fat, vitamins and minerals.

The easiest way to plan their diet is by using the Children's Food Guide Pyramid, shown on page 4. It divides food into seven groups based on the nutritional recommendations of the World Health Organisation, and tells you how many portions of each food group children should aim to have each day. The foods at the bottom of the pyramid should make up the largest proportion of their diet while the foods at the top of the pyramid should be eaten in smaller amounts.

Make sure you:

- Include foods from each food group in the pyramid every day
- Choose a variety of foods from each group
- Provide the recommended number of portions from each food group each day
- Check the portion sizes suggested overleaf.

Approximate Daily Nutritional Needs of Children

FOOD GROUP	NUMBER OF PORTIONS EACH DAY	FOOD	PORTION SIZE (5–8 YEARS)	PORTION SIZE (9–12 YEARS)
Vegetables	3		The amount a child can hold in their hand	
		Broccoli, cauliflower	1–2 spears/floret	2–3 spears/florets
		Carrots	1 small carrot	1 carrot
		Peas	2 tablespoons	3 tablespoons
		Other vegetables	2 tablespoons	3 tablespoons
		Tomatoes	3 cherry tomatoes	5 cherry tomatoes
Fruit	2		The amount a child can hold in their hand	
		Apple, pear, peach, banana	1 small fruit	1 medium fruit
		Plum, kiwi fruit, satsuma	1 fruit	1–2 fruit
		Strawberries	6	8–10
		Grapes	8–12	12–16
		Tinned fruit	2 tablespoons	3 tablespoons
		Fruit juice	1 small glass	1 medium glass
Grains and Potatoes	4–6		The size of a child's fist	
		Bread	1 small slice	1 slice
		Rolls/muffins	1/2 roll	1 roll
		Pasta or rice	3 tablespoons	4 tablespoons
		Breakfast cereal	3 tablespoons	4 tablespoons
		Potatoes, sweet potatoes, yams	1 fist-sized	1 fist-sized
Calcium-rich foods	2	Milk (dairy or calcium-fortified soya milk)	1 small cup	1 medium cup
		Cheese	Size of 4 dice	Size of 4 dice
		Tofu	Size of 4 dice	Size of 4 dice
		Tinned sardines	1 tablespoon	1–2 tablespoons
		Yoghurt/fromage frais	1 pot	1 pot
Protein-rich foods	2		Size of a child's palm	
		Lean meat	1 slice (40 g)	1–2 slices (40–80 g)
		Poultry	2 thin slices/1 small breast	2 medium slices/1 breast
		Fish	Half a fillet	1 fillet
		Egg	1	1–2
		Lentils/beans	2 tablespoons	3 tablespoons
		Tofu/soya burger or sausage	1 small	1 medium
Healthy fats and oils	1	Nuts and seeds	1 tablespoon	1 heaped tablespoon
		Seed oils, nut oils	2 teaspoons	1 tablespoon
		Oily fish*	60 g (2 oz)	85 g (3 oz)

*Oily fish is very rich in essential fats so just 1 portion a week would more than cover a child's daily needs

How many portions a day?

Try to include the suggested number of portions of each food group each day. Remember, these are guidelines and on some days children may need more or less of a certain food group.

Grains and potatoes

Bread, pasta, rice, noodles, breakfast cereals, porridge oats, crackers, potatoes, sweet potatoes, parsnips and yams.
Benefits: Rich energy sources, providing essential B vitamins, iron and other minerals and an important source of fibre for a healthy digestive system.

Fruit and vegetables

Benefits: Rich sources of many vitamins and minerals and other plant nutrients (phytonutrients), which are important for health and fighting off illnesses.

Calcium-rich foods

Milk, soya milk (fortified with calcium), cheese, yoghurt, fromage frais, tofu, tinned fish with edible bones (e.g. sardines), dark green leafy vegetables.
Benefits: Rich sources of calcium, which is important for building healthy bones and teeth.

Protein-rich foods

Lean meat, chicken, turkey, fish, eggs, beans, lentils, nuts, and soya and quorn products.
Benefits: Important sources of protein, which is needed for growth and development. Protein-rich foods also provide B vitamins, iron and zinc.

WHAT ABOUT VEGETARIANS?

You may substitute extra dairy food for one of the portions in the protein-rich group, as dairy foods are also rich in protein. For example, aim for three portions of dairy foods plus one portion of protein-rich foods. However, don't eliminate this group entirely as these foods supply valuable vitamins and minerals not present in dairy foods.

Tip *Try to include mostly unrefined or wholegrain foods in your child's diet as they contain more vitamins, minerals and fibre than 'white' or refined varieties.*

Tip *Provide as much variety as possible. Aim for a mix of colours: orange/yellow, red, green, purple and white*

Tip *Use lean cuts of meat and limit sausages, burgers and nuggets to no more than two portions a week because they contain a lot of saturated fat and salt.*

Tip *Even if your family isn't vegetarian, try to introduce some vegetable protein foods (beans, lentils and soya) into your children's diet. These foods provide a unique type of fibre that's beneficial for the digestive system, as well as important plant nutrients.*

fatty and sugary foods
up to 1 portion a day
or in moderation

healthy fats and oils
1–2 portions a day

protein-rich foods
2–4 portions a day

calcium-rich foods
2–4 portions a day

grains and potatoes
4–6 portions a day

vegetables
3–5
portions
a day

fruit
2–4
portions
a day

Healthy fats and oils

Nuts (walnuts, cashews, almonds, pecans, Brazils, pine nuts), seeds (sesame, pumpkin, sunflower), seed and nut oils (e.g. olive, rapeseed, sunflower), and oily fish (e.g. sardines, mackerel, pilchards).
Benefits: Excellent sources of essential fats (omega-3 and omega-6 fats) and monounsaturated fats, essential for health. The omega-3 fats are important for brain development and normal eyesight.

Fatty and sugary foods

Biscuits, cakes, sweets, confectionery, soft drinks, chocolate, crisps and other savoury snacks.

These are high in saturated fat, added sugar and/or salt. They provide lots of calories but few, if any, essential nutrients ('empty calories').

 Try to limit these foods to one portion daily.

NUT ALLERGIES

Nuts can cause serious allergies in a small proportion of children and peanuts seem to cause the worst reaction. The exact cause is not known but children with nut allergies often have other allergies and other allergy-related conditions such as asthma, hay fever and eczema. A family history of allergy also increases the risk of a child developing a nut allergy. Early signs may include a mild tingling in the mouth or more obvious swelling in the mouth, difficulty in breathing, and swallowing, culminating, occasionally, in anaphylactic shock, which can kill if not dealt with quickly.

It is recommended that young children under three years old with a family history of allergy should not be given peanuts in any form. Children with no allergy history can be given peanuts and other nut products after the age of one. Whole nuts should not be given to children under five years old because of the risk of choking but they can be used finely ground or as peanut butter.

HOW BIG IS A PORTION?

The exact portion size depends on the child's age, weight, size and energy needs. In general, younger children need fewer calories than older children so offer them smaller amounts. In the main, be guided by your child's appetite. Remember it's the overall balance of foods that is most important. See the table on page 2 for guidelines.

PERFECTLY BALANCED SALAD

This salad is an almost perfectly balanced meal. It includes foods from each food group – peppers and salad leaves from the vegetables group, raisins and apples from the fruit group, pasta from the cereal and potatoes group, nuts and yoghurt from the calcium-rich food group, red kidney beans and nuts from the protein-rich foods group, and low-fat mayonnaise from the healthy fats group.

Makes 4 servings
- 125 g (4 oz) pasta shells
- ½ red pepper
- ½ yellow pepper
- 60 g (2 oz) toasted flaked almonds, cashews or peanuts
- 60 g (2 oz) raisins
- 125 g (4 oz) cooked or canned red kidney beans
- 2 tomatoes, sliced
- 1 apple, sliced
- Mixed salad leaves, e.g. watercress, rocket, endive or baby spinach

For the dressing:
- 3 tbsp (45 ml) low-fat mayonnaise

1. Cook the pasta shells according to directions on the packet. Drain.
2. Mix the pasta with the peppers, nuts, raisins, beans, tomatoes and apple slices.
3. Arrange the salad leaves on a serving dish. Pile the pasta mixture on top.
4. Combine the low-fat mayonnaise with the salad.

Salt

We should all avoid eating too much salt, whatever our age. This is because salt contains sodium and having too much sodium can cause raised blood pressure, which increases the risk of heart disease and stroke.

It's important to keep an eye on how much salt your child is consuming. How much is too much? Children under seven should have no more than 3 g of salt a day. Those between seven and ten should have no more than 5 g daily and those aged 11+ no more than 6 g daily.

Children are particularly vulnerable to the effects of salt, but despite requiring less salt than adults, the average child in the UK consumes as much (10–12 g /day).

Lots of processed foods are high in salt, including many products aimed at children. So you might not realise how much salt your child is eating. Processed foods include everything from breakfast cereals and biscuits to soups and tinned spaghetti. A small can of pasta shapes and mini sausages in tomato sauce contains 2.5 g of salt, almost the entire recommended daily maximum for six-year old children. And a cheeseburger with a small portion of fries contains 3.3 g salt, which is 10% more than the daily maximum intake.

How to reduce their salt intake

- Limit tinned foods, such as pasta shapes in tomato sauce and baked beans. Buy reduced salt versions (although they are still quite high in salt and may contain artificial sweeteners too) or remove some of the sauce.

- Cut down on burgers, sausages and chicken nuggets – one portion contains around half of their daily salt maximum.

- Limit the number of salty snacks such as crisps and biscuits. Instead, give them low-salt snacks, such as dried fruit, raw vegetable sticks, grapes and satsumas.

- Check labels on food to check how much salt is listed on the packaging. Try to choose foods that contain just a little sodium: **0.1 g or less per 100 g**.

- Cut down on ready-made sauces – one portion of pasta sauce contains around one third of a child's daily maximum.

- Look for bread with lower levels of salt or those made with salt replacer. Two slices of ordinary bread contain around 1 g salt.

- Make your own soup – ready-made tinned or fresh soup contains up to 2.5 g salt per portion.

- Make sure they have plenty of fruit and vegetables, which are rich in the mineral potassium which helps balance out some of the harmful effects of salt.

AGE	MAXIMUM DAILY SALT INTAKE*
4–6 years	3 g
7–10 years	5 g
11 + years	6 g

* Recommendations from the Food Standards Agency, May 2003.

SALT CONTENT OF VARIOUS FOODS (PER TYPICAL CHILD'S PORTION)

Chicken nuggets	1.8 g
Pizza	1.3 g
Can of beans	2.5 g
Doughnut	1.2 g
Hamburger	2.0 g
Milk shake	0.5 g
Frosties cereal	1.5 g
Cheese or ham Lunchable pack	2.4 g
Can of spaghetti	2.3 g
2 fish fingers	1.3 g
Pasta sauce	1.0 g
Crisps	0.6 g
Shepherd's pie ready meal	1.9 g

CHECK THE LABEL

To see if a product is high in salt, according to the Food Standards Agency recommendations, compare the amount per 100 g with the following guidelines

SALT: More than 1.25 g is high

Less than 0.25 g is low

SODIUM: More than 0.5 g is high

Less than 0.1 g is low

One gram of sodium is equivalent to 2.5 g of salt.

Sugar

Foods and drinks containing sugar shouldn't be eaten too often as they can contribute to tooth decay. They also tend to be high in calories and fat and low in other valuable nutrients. As a result, a high-sugar diet is often linked with obesity.

The World Health Organisation recommends that adults and children should get no more than 10% of daily calories from sugar. But, on average, British children get around 17% of their daily energy needs from sugar – considerably higher than the recommended maximum.

Ideally, children aged 4–6 years should eat no more than 40 g (2½ tablespoons) a day, 7–10 years olds no more than 46 g (3 tablespoons) and 11–14 year olds no more than 50 g (3½ tablespoons).

Sugar doesn't just come from obvious foods such as soft drinks, biscuits, cakes, sweets, chocolate and desserts. Yoghurt, ready meals, breakfast cereals, sauces and baked beans contain high levels of added sugar (see Sugar Guide). Check labels for names such as sucrose, glucose syrup, dextrose, fruit syrup and glucose. They're all forms of sugar and all can be harmful to teeth!

CHECK THE LABEL

To see if a product is high in sugar according to the Food Standards Agency recommendations, compare the amount per 100 g with the following guidelines
More than 10 g is high
Less than 2 g is low
Caution! No added sugar doesn't mean the food is low in sugar – it may contain other ingredients such as fruit juice with a high natural sugar content.

WATCH THE POP

Children drink an average of six cans of fizzy drinks a week – that's twice as much as 15 years ago.

How to cut down on sugar

- Don't ban sweets and chocolate completely – limit them to certain clearly defined occasions. For example, allow one 'treat' every Saturday after supper. If your children are given sweets on other days, they can save them for Saturday.

- Keep any food and drink containing sugar mainly to mealtimes to reduce the risk of tooth decay.

- Check the labels for hidden sugars – glucose syrup, dextrose – and try to choose foods that contain less than 2 g sugar per 100 g.

- Limit soft drinks, sweets, biscuits, cakes and puddings. Even artificially sweetened varieties encourage a liking for sugar.

- Don't add unnecessary sugar to food.

- Use more unprocessed foods that are naturally sweet – fresh and dried fruit – they contain more vitamins and fibre.

- Give plain water to drink. If your children aren't keen on it, give fruit juice diluted with water – you can gradually add less juice and more water.

AGE	MAXIMUM DAILY SUGAR INTAKE
4–6 years	40 g (2½ tablespoons)
7–10 years	46 g (3 tablespoons)
11 + years	50 g (3½ tablespoons)

SUGAR GUIDE

Can of cola	7 teaspoons
Glass of fruit drink or Sunny D	4 teaspoons
Chocolate bar	8 teaspoons
2 biscuits	2 teaspoons
1 tablespoon tomato ketchup	1 teaspoon
Small can of baked beans/pasta shapes	2 teaspoons
2 scoops ice-cream	4½ teaspoons
1 pot of fruit yoghurt	3 teaspoons
Small bowl of Frosties	3 teaspoons
Small bowl of Coco Pops	3 teaspoons
1 breakfast cereal bar	2 teaspoons
1 fruit snack roll (Winders)	3 teaspoons

Q&A

Question: Is it better to give children sugar-free products that contain artificial sweeteners instead of sugar?

Answer: Artificial sweeteners, such as aspartame acesulphane K and saccharin, may not decay children's teeth but they still encourage intensely sweet tastes. The government considers them safe – although they're not allowed in baby foods – but some scientists argue that high intakes may be linked with migraines and brain tumours. In moderation, there's probably little danger to children's health. But why not get sweetness from fresh or dried fruit or just have small amounts of sweet foods, such as good chocolate, which has no artificial sweeteners?

Looking after children's teeth

Eating lots of sugary foods increase the chances of tooth decay, especially if children eat them frequently throughout the day. Fruit, fruit juice, fruit drinks and squash can also cause enamel erosion – literally dissolving the tooth away – because they contain fruit acids. Here's what you can do to help prevent tooth decay and erosion.

- Encourage children to brush their teeth with a little fluoride toothpaste twice a day, after breakfast and before bed, and shortly after eating sugary foods.

- Milk is a far 'safer' drink for teeth. Fruit juice diluted at least 1 part juice to 1 part water is better than squash, fruit drinks and fizzy drinks.

- Discourage sugary or sticky foods – sweets, chocolate, biscuits, raisins and other dried fruit and fruit bars – between meals. These leave residues on the teeth, increasing the risk of decay. Note: dried fruit is as potentially harmful to teeth as sweets!

- If sugary foods or drinks are eaten, then it is better to finish them quickly than sucking a packet of sweets or sipping a drink for an hour or more.

- Encourage the drinking of acidic drinks with a straw. This reduces the contact of the drink with the teeth. Sugar-free drinks aren't necessarily better for children's teeth as they are quite acidic and can cause dental erosion.

- Eating a small piece of cheese at the end of a meal or after a sugary or acidic snack helps counteract the harmful effects of sugar. *Cheese is alkali and rich in calcium and neutralises the fruit acids.*

Fruit is a natural source of sugar, but fruit also contains fibre and vitamins that balance out the sugar.

RASPBERRY FOOL

This dessert contains no added sugar; the sweetness is provided by a little honey and the natural sugars in the raspberries. It is also packed with vitamin C. You can substitute other seasonal fruits such as strawberries, blackberries or, in the winter, mango or stewed apple.

Makes 4 servings
- 225 g (8 oz) raspberries
- 225 g (8 oz) low-fat plain fromage frais
- 1 tbsp (15 ml) clear honey

1 Mash the raspberries lightly with a fork.

2 Mix with the fromage frais and honey. Spoon into 4 bowls.

Q&A

Question: What are the healthiest drinks to give children?

Answer: The best drinks to give children are water, milk and milkshakes with no added sugar. Fruit juice is also a healthy drink – it contains valuable vitamins and minerals and can count as one portion a day towards the five-a day target – but should be diluted at least one to one with water. Juice contains natural sugars that can damage teeth, especially if your children sip it from a bottle or drink it frequently. So, try to keep fruit juice to mealtimes. This is better for teeth than drinking it between meals.

Squash, juice drinks, fizzy drinks, flavoured milks and milkshakes contain added sugar, which is also bad for teeth. Diluting squash well will make it less sugary, but again try to keep it to mealtimes.

All fizzy drinks, including 'diet' varieties, contain very few nutrients. And they can also be very filling, so they could reduce your children's appetite for food that contains the nutrients they need.

SNACKS AND DRINKS THAT ARE SAFER FOR TEETH

SNACKS	DRINKS
▪ Fresh fruit	▪ Water
▪ Yoghurt (preferably unsweetened)	▪ Milk
▪ Cheese (with crackers or bread)	▪ Diluted fruit juice (1 or 2 parts water to 1 part juice)
▪ Toast, plain or with Marmite, peanut butter or cheese	
▪ Nuts	
▪ Crudités with dips	
▪ Savoury sandwiches	

Summary

- If children learn to enjoy a balanced diet now, they'll continue to eat well and stay healthy, as they get older.

- Keep to the 80/20 rule – if children eat a balanced diet around 80% of the time, they're free to enjoy other foods they want the other 20% of the time.

- Each day children should aim to have 5 portions of fruit and vegetables; 4–6 portions of grains and potatoes, 2 portions of protein-rich foods, 2 portions of calcium-rich foods and 1 portion of healthy fats.

- Keep an eye on how much salt your child is having – limit to 3–6 g daily (depending on age).

- Limit foods and drinks containing sugar to 40–50 g daily (depending on age); they can contribute to tooth decay and obesity and displace other nutrients in the diet.

- Water, milk or diluted fruit juice are healthier options for teeth.

BANANA MILKSHAKE

This simple, nutritious shake includes no added sugar and is much better for teeth than sugary drinks.

Makes 2 servings

- 250 ml (8 fl oz) milk (full-fat or semi-skimmed)
- 2 ripe bananas, sliced
- Few ice cubes, crushed

1 Put the milk, crushed ice and banana in a blender. Blend until smooth, thick and bubbly.

How to get kids to eat fruit and vegetables

Getting children to eat the five portions of fruit and vegetables a day recommended by the World Health Organisation and the UK's Food Standards Agency can be a struggle. On average, children in the UK only eat two portions of fruit and veg a day – that's way short of the recommended amount!

This means that many are almost certainly missing out on important nutrients. As well as being a great source of fibre, fruit and vegetables are rich in vitamins (especially disease-fighting vitamins A and C), minerals and other important plant nutrients, which help keep children healthy and boost their immunity.

What's a portion?

A child portion is roughly the amount they can hold in their hand – their portion grows as they do! This could be:

Fruit

- 1 small apple, pear, banana or peach
- About 12 grapes
- 1 satsuma, kiwi fruit or plum
- About 6–7 strawberries
- A glass of pure fruit juice
- 2–3 tablespoons tinned fruit
- One tablespoon of raisins, sultanas, dried apricots or dried mango

Veg

- 2 tablespoons of peas, cabbage or sweetcorn
- 2 broccoli spears
- 1 cooked carrot or 7–8 carrot sticks
- 3–5 cherry tomatoes
- 7–8 cucumber slices

5-a-day can be achieved by:

Menu 1

1. A glass of orange juice with breakfast
2. Grapes or banana as a snack
3. Pizza topped with extra vegetables for lunch
4. A portion of carrots at teatime
5. Fruit mixed with yoghurt for pudding

Menu 2

1. Breakfast cereal topped with banana slices
2. An apple as a snack
3. Vegetable soup for lunch
4. Carrot, pepper and cucumber sticks or cherry tomatoes at teatime
5. Apple crumble for pudding

Why 5 a day?

- Children will be less likely to get minor infections such as colds and flu if they eat plenty of fruit and veg – particularly those rich in vitamin C, such as oranges, kiwi fruit, red peppers, strawberries and raspberries.

- Five daily portions of fruit and veg help protect against many cancers in later life.

- A high level of fruit and veg in the diet cuts the risk of heart disease and stroke during adulthood.

Ideally, aim for 2 portions of fruit and 3 portions of vegetables. Variety is key. Mix colours – green, orange, red, yellow, purple – as each colour provides different health benefits.

Tip *Try adding vegetables to sauces, soups and pies.* *Vegetables such as chopped carrots, mushrooms and peppers can be added to Bolognese sauce, vegetable soup, lasagne, hot pots, stews, bakes and pies. The tomato in pasta sauce counts as a portion, but try adding a cupful of chopped broccoli, peppers, courgettes or mushrooms.*

Five ways to eat 5

One
Most children eat 3 meals and 2 snacks a day. If they have 1 portion of fruit or vegetables at each eating occasion, they've hit 5-a-day!

Two
Use the Rainbow Rule: Every day try to get your child to eat 5 different colours of fruit or vegetables.

Three
Set a good example yourself. Children are more likely to eat fruit and vegetables if they see you enjoying these foods daily and if there's a plentiful supply in the house.

Four
Use a star reward chart to meet their 5-a-day target, giving one star for each daily portion of fruit and veg.

Five
Get children involved with the shopping – let them choose a new variety of fruit and vegetable (and then, hopefully, eat it!).

Q&A

Question: The only vegetable my child seems to want is potatoes – in the form of chips. How can I make his diet more varied?

Answer: Unfortunately, potatoes don't count towards the 5-a-day target for fruit and veg – they contain fewer vitamins so are regarded as carbohydrate foods.

Instead of always using potatoes, how about making oven chips from other root vegetables? Cut sweet potatoes, carrots, parsnips, swede, butternut squash or pumpkin into wedges, toss in a little olive or rapeseed oil and pop in the oven at 200°C (400°F or Gas mark 6) for 25–30 minutes.

CARROT SOUP

This soup is inexpensive and simple to make, and packed with the antioxidant beta-carotene (which the body converts into vitamin A) and which helps fight disease.

Makes 4 servings
- 2 tbsp (30 ml) olive oil
- 1 onion, chopped
- 1 clove of garlic, crushed
- 675 g (1½ lb) carrots, sliced
- 900 ml (1½ pints) vegetable stock*
- Salt and freshly ground black pepper
- 1–2 tablespoons fresh coriander, chopped (optional)

*Alternatively, use 3 tsp (15 ml) Swiss vegetable bouillon or 1½ vegetable stock cubes in 900 ml (1½ pints) water

1 Sauté the onion and garlic in the olive oil for 5 minutes in a large saucepan.

2 Add the carrots and continue cooking for a further 2 minutes.

3 Add the stock and bring to the boil, then reduce the heat and simmer for 15 minutes or until the carrots are tender.

4 Season with the salt and pepper and add the fresh coriander.

5 Liquidise using a hand blender or food processor.

How to make vegetables fun for kids

Do your children struggle to eat their vegetables or refuse to eat anything 'green'? If vegetables aren't included as part of a meal, they'll be missing out on a concentrated source of vitamins and minerals and almost certainly fill up with more pudding, or ask for snacks later on when they get hungry.

Grow your own vegetables

Children will enjoy helping to grow vegetables. Help them plant and harvest their own vegetable garden. Almost any patch of garden soil will do or use a large tray or pot filled with compost. The easiest to grow are potatoes, runner beans, tomatoes, spinach and courgettes. Think of it as a valuable educational experience as children will learn exactly where vegetables come from (not the supermarket!).

Get them in the kitchen

Let your children help wash, peel and cut vegetables. When they feel involved with meal planning and preparation, they're more likely to try new vegetables.

Don't force it

Won't eat spinach or sprouts? Don't fret if your children won't eat a wide range of vegetables. They can get the key nutrients – vitamin C and beta-carotene – from strawberries and carrots. As their tastes develop, they will start to like other vegetables.

Add vegetables to pizzas

Let children decorate their own pizzas with a selection of peppers, sweetcorn, courgettes, mushrooms, tomatoes and pineapple. Or mix finely chopped or pureed vegetables into the tomato sauce before topping the pizza base.

Hide 'em

You can get children to try a new vegetable if you mix it with a food they already like, such as mashed potato (try adding swede, parsnip, cabbage or spinach), soup, curry or macaroni cheese.

Let them choose

Children like to decide on their own portions so put out dishes and big spoons and let them serve themselves. They're more likely to eat the portion they've chosen than one you've served them!

Start small

If you do serve food straight on to your children's plate, put out tiny portions of two or three vegetables. Large portions can look overwhelming and may not get eaten at all. Children are more likely to eat small portions of two or three different vegetables than one large portion.

Eat 'em raw

Carrot and cucumber sticks, pepper strips, baby sweetcorn and cherry tomatoes make tasty lunchbox foods or teatime nibbles. Serve with hummus, salsa or a cheesy dip. Younger children who refuse most vegetables will often eat 'finger' vegetables.

Try frozen

If you don't always have time to chop vegetables, use pre-prepared or frozen varieties instead. Many frozen vegetables such as peas are just as nutritious as fresh versions as they're frozen within hours of picking.

Make them attractive

For younger children, try to make vegetables more fun – arrange broccoli and cauliflower as trees on a base of mashed potato; make faces (e.g. use carrots for eyes, baby sweetcorn for a nose, red peppers for the mouth, broccoli for hair, or whatever else your child likes!).

Q&A

Question: My children say vegetables are boring and always moan at the sight of them on their plate.

Answer: Jazz up plain vegetables with a little grated cheese or tomato ketchup. Or combine with a home-made or ready-bought sauce. Broccoli, cauliflower and Brussels sprouts go well with cheese sauce; beans, peas and sweetcorn can be stirred into pasta sauce. Slather salad with a low fat dressing or creamy dip. Forget meat and two veg. All-in-one dishes transform vegetables into meals in their own right: think vegetable curry, vegetable hot pot and vegetable chilli.

Pack one portion of fruit in your child's lunchbox. This could be an apple, plum, a few grapes or cherries, a banana, a satsuma or a small ring-pull can or carton of fruit. On school outings, my eldest daughter loves halving a kiwi with a plastic knife then scooping out the flesh with a plastic spoon.

Think tomatoes

Tomato-based pasta sauce as well as tomato soup, tinned tomatoes and passata (pureed tomatoes) count as one portion. Tomatoes are a great source of antioxidants, especially lycopene, which help protect against heart disease and cancer. Add extra vegetables – frozen peas, sweetcorn, mushrooms, or tinned red kidney beans.

KEEP THE VITAMINS IN!

- Buy locally grown produce if you can, ideally from farm shops and local markets. This means the vitamins are less likely to be lost between being picked and being served!

- Buy British if you have a choice – imported produce is usually harvested under-ripe (before it has developed its full vitamin quota) and will have lost much of its nutritional value during its journey to your supermarket.

- Buy fresh-looking, unblemished, undamaged fruit and vegetables.

- Prepare fruit and vegetables just before you make them into a salad or cook them. From the moment they are chopped they start to lose nutrients.

- Fruit and vegetables should be eaten unpeeled wherever possible – many vitamins and minerals are concentrated just beneath the skin.

- Use frozen food if fresh is not available – it's nutritionally similar.

- Cut into large pieces rather than small; vitamins are lost from cut surfaces.

- Steam or boil vegetables in the minimum amount of water to preserve the vitamins.

- When boiling vegetables, add to fast-boiling water and cook as briefly as possible until they're tender-crisp, not soft and mushy.

- Save the cooking water for soups, stocks and sauces.

- Don't re-heat leftover cooked vegetables – they'll have lost most of their nutritional value.

How to make fruit fun

Grow them

If you have the space, try planting an apple, pear or plum tree – children will enjoy the experience of observing the yearly cycle of a fruit tree. Strawberries can be grown in tubs and produce lots of fruit.

Make snacks healthy

Establish nutritious snack habits; make fresh fruit the norm for at least one snack a day. Apple slices, grapes and peeled satsumas are all good choices.

Start early

Get them to have one fruit portion at breakfast. Top breakfast cereal with sliced bananas, grated apple or a handful of raisins.

Eat dessert first

If your children are too hungry to wait for supper, give them dessert first – apple slices, grapes, melon – to stave off their hunger pangs and help reach their 5-a-day target.

Tip *If I find strawberries or other summer fruit lacking in flavour, I let my children sprinkle on a little sugar. After a few minutes, the sugar will have dissolved on the fruit surface and brought out a nice flavour.*

Q&A

Question: How can I persuade my children to snack on fruit instead of biscuits?

Answer: Fruit, cut into bite-sized pieces, will be more attractive than whole fruit for younger children. Make a fruit platter of bite-sized pieces of fruit and let your children dig in.

   If your children must snack in front of the television, give them a bowl of grapes, cherries or sliced apples. Without realising it, my daughters often get through a couple of fruit portions while watching their favourite programme.

Drink fruit

Fruit smoothies and shakes are a delicious way to get a portion or two of fruit. Liquidise fresh or tinned fruit (such as strawberries, mango or bananas) with fruit juice and/or yoghurt or milk.

STRAWBERRY SHAKE

Strawberries are an excellent source of vitamin C.

Makes 2 servings

- 150 ml (¼ pint) milk (full-fat or semi-skimmed)
- 1 × 125 g carton low-fat strawberry yoghurt
- 1 handful of strawberries
- Few ice cubes, crushed

1 Put the milk, crushed ice and strawberries in a blender. Blend until smooth, thick and bubbly.

Make fruit salad together

Let them choose their own fruit combinations. Younger children can peel bananas and satsumas, or prepare grapes; older children can chop and slice plums, apples and peaches.

Keep it varied

Children can easily get bored with the same fruit (such as apples and bananas). Try to eat a different fruit at least once a week. Enjoy the fruits of the seasons by choosing strawberries, raspberries and peaches in the summer, blackberries and plums in the autumn, grapes and clementines in the winter.

Have a dessert

Puddings can be healthy. Try fruit kebabs (threaded onto cocktail sticks or wooden skewers), banana custard, baked apples stuffed with raisins, baked bananas with chocolate (see recipe below), fresh or tinned fruit mixed with yoghurt, rice pudding with stewed apples, dried apricots, or fresh raspberries, and apple crumble. See the recipes on pp 117–21.

Display fruit

If fruit is on display – say in a fruit bowl – in a place your children can easily reach, they're more likely to grab them as they go past.

Make fruit look terrific

When preparing a fruit arrangement or fruit salad, think of colour combinations. Try to contrast two or three different coloured fruit, such as strawberries with bite-sized pieces of Galia melon; blackberries with sliced peaches; mix red and green grapes. Arrange fruit in simple patterns: orange segments in a star shape; alternate plum and nectarine slices; banana slices around the rim of a plate with kiwi slices in the centre. Or let your children make their own patterns.

Mix with yoghurt

Mix berries or chopped soft fruit such as bananas with plain or fruit yoghurt. Alternatively, layer chopped or mashed fruit with yoghurt in tall sundae glasses.

Dried fruit is a healthy snack but can stick to the teeth, making it as potentially harmful as sweets. Follow with a drink of water and a small piece of cheese. Or encourage tooth-brushing shortly afterwards.

BAKED BANANAS WITH CHOCOLATE BUTTONS

Makes 4 servings

- 4 bananas
- Chocolate buttons

1 Preheat the oven to 200 °C/400 °F/Gas mark 6.

2 Peel the bananas. Make a slit lengthwise in each banana, not quite cutting all the way through.

3 Insert the chocolate buttons in the banana slits. Wrap each banana loosely in foil and place on a baking tray.

4 Bake in the oven for 15 minutes. Unwrap the foil parcels when cool enough and the bananas will be oozing with delicious chocolate sauce!

Make fruit lollies

Make fruit lollies or 'ice cream' by freezing one of the following mixtures in plastic lolly moulds or little fromage frais pots (insert a wooden lolly stick when half-frozen):

- Pureed strawberries
- Mashed raspberries mixed with an equal amount of raspberry yoghurt
- Pureed mango
- Mashed banana

Flip a pancake

Not just for Pancake Day. Try filling pancakes with sliced bananas; tinned pineapple; sliced mango; thawed frozen summer fruits; crushed raspberries . . . the possibilities are endless (see recipe page 117).

BANANA ICE

Good source of fibre, vitamin C, vitamin B6.

Makes 2 child portions

Storage: 3 months in the freezer; do not re-freeze

Preparation: 5 minutes

- 2 ripe bananas

1 Peel and mash the bananas. Transfer to a small plastic container. Cover and place in the freezer for several hours.

2 Allow it to stand at room temperature for 10 minutes before serving.

3 Serve in bowls or in ice cream cones.

Fruit contains natural fruit acids, which can over time dissolve the tooth enamel. Serve a cheese with fruit at mealtimes or follow eating fruit with a small piece of cheese. Cheese is alkali and rich in calcium and neutralises the fruit acids.

Fruit bars and fruit snack rolls are marketed as healthy alternatives to fruit but are far removed from the fresh version and can be very harmful to the teeth. The main ingredients – concentrated fruit juice and puree – are almost pure sugar, and these are supplemented with extra sugar, fruit acids, flavours and colours. Nothing healthy about these. Worse, the bars stick to the teeth, making them just as damaging as sweets.

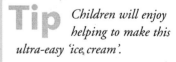 Tip *Children will enjoy helping to make this ultra-easy 'ice cream'.*

Summary

■ Five portions of fruit and vegetables a day are recommended to help keep children healthy, fight off illnesses and protect them from heart disease and cancer in later life.

■ Set a good example – children are more likely to eat fruit and vegetables if they see you enjoying these foods daily and if there's a plentiful supply in the house.

■ Don't worry too much if they don't like many vegetables. Stick with the ones they will eat – they can get the key nutrients from extra fruit.

■ Unpopular vegetables can often be disguised – in soup, curry, pies, casseroles, pizza toppings or pasta sauce – and then new vegetables gradually introduced with a food they already like.

■ If possible, try growing your own fruit and vegetables and getting children involved with meal planning and preparation – they'll be more likely to eat the fruit and vegetables.

■ Establish healthy snack habits, making fresh fruit the norm for at least one snack daily. Make fruit and vegetables fun by presenting them in interesting shapes, smaller (but more) portions, attractive colour combinations and in delicious recipes.

The weight issue

Although chubbiness in babies and toddlers is regarded as normal – desirable even – as a child gets older, being overweight can put his or her health at risk. According to the Government's Health Survey for England, as many as one in three children are overweight and one in ten is obese. That's three times more than 10 years ago.

Experts are talking about a looming epidemic of obesity, and predict that by 2020 one in four boys and one in three girls aged 7–11 will be overweight or obese.

Being a chubby is no fun. Plus, apart from being more likely to be teased, bullied and suffer from low self-esteem, overweight children are more likely to develop:

- Bone and joint problems (due to excess weight)

- Breathing problems and asthma

- High blood pressure, high blood cholesterol, type 2 diabetes and artery damage during their teens and early adulthood

- Heart disease and stroke in later life

Most seriously, overweight children are likely to grow up to become fat adults.

The Big Question: What makes children put on weight?

The reason why children become overweight is simple; they consume more calories than they burn. Unfortunately the reason *why* they overeat isn't so straightforward.

A child's personality, home life, relationships and lifestyle affect how much and what he or she eats, as well as the amount of daily activity he or she takes. The truth is today's busy lifestyles make it harder for children to follow a healthy diet than 10 years ago.

> Type 2 diabetes, previously linked to obesity in middle age, is being increasingly diagnosed in teenagers.

Obesity has trebled in children aged 6 to 15 between 1990 and 2001, from 5% to 16%. One in every 10 pre-school child is obese.

Why do some children overeat?

- These days there's an abundance of **foods laden with fat, sugar and salt.**

- **Snacks** are now staple parts of many children's diets. Grazing and snacking rather than eating balanced meals tends to be the norm.

- **Bigger portions and supersize marketing** – especially for snacks and fast foods – means that many children have lost track of normal portion sizes.

- **Marketing and advertising** of fast foods and certain snacks is often aimed at children, and influences what they choose to eat.

- Children spend more time in front of the **television and computer** nowadays. This means they're less active and watch more adverts tempting them towards unhealthy foods.

- Parents lead **busier lives** and so have less time to cook. Many find it easier to feed children ready meals and fast foods.

- Most **children's menus** in restaurants offer foods laden with fat, salt and sugar.

- **Food and drink in schools** is usually poor quality and loaded with fat, sugar and salt. Most children tend to choose fast food and chips for school meals. Plus many schools have vending machines selling calorie-laden snacks and drinks.

- **Changes in family meal patterns** mean that children are more likely to eat in front of the television or on the run.

Hamburgers are 112% larger, pasta servings 480% larger and chocolate chip cookies 700% bigger than 20 years ago.

Big Problems: Choccie and chips

Fast food and sugary and salty snacks can fool children into eating more calories than their body needs. They are 'energy dense', which means they contain a lot of calories for a small amount of food. The Medical Research Council found that a typical fast food meal had more than one and a half times the calories of a similar-sized portion of a traditional British meal.

On the move? Children and exercise

- Children lead inactive lives these days, and spend too much time sitting down. The Health Survey of England found that half of all children do not meet their minimum physical activity target (1 hour on at least 5 days each week).

- Schools have reduced the time spent on PE; Sport England found that only one in three primary school children receive the recommended 2 hours of PE per week.

- Children are more likely to get driven to school these days – twenty years ago, 80 per cent of children walked or cycled to school. Compare this with the mere 5 per cent of children today.

IS YOUR CHILD OVERWEIGHT OR OBESE?

Your child's body mass index (BMI) indicates whether they're a healthy weight. To calculate your child's body mass index (BMI), divide the child's weight (in kilograms) by the square of the child's height (in metres). Then check the chart opposite. A BMI higher than the normal limit for their age means they are overweight, a BMI higher than the obese value suggests their health is at risk.

$BMI = weight (kg)/height (m)^2$

For example, a child weighing 45 kg and measuring 1.4 m:

$45/(1.4 \times 1.4) = 22.9$

$BMI = 22.9$.

BMIS FOR OVERWEIGHT OR OBESE CHILDREN

AGE	OVERWEIGHT		OBESE	
	BOYS	GIRLS	BOYS	GIRLS
5	17.4	17.1	19.3	19.2
6	17.6	17.3	19.8	19.7
7	17.9	17.8	20.6	20.5
8	18.4	18.3	21.6	21.6
9	19.1	19.1	22.8	22.8
10	19.8	19.9	24.0	24.1
11	20.6	20.7	25.1	25.4
12	21.2	21.7	26.0	26.7
13	21.9	22.6	26.8	27.8

The healthy way to fight obesity

What's the solution? No one wants to see their child on fad diets, ruining their health. But at the same time, you can't sit back and do nothing. The best approach is to encourage a balanced diet and regular physical activity. Talk to your child about healthy eating and exercise, teach by example and guide your child – but at the same time let your child make his or her own decisions about food.

Healthy mind, healthy body: Building self-esteem

If you boost your child's self-esteem and help them feel more positive about themselves they're more likely to make healthier food choices. Make a point of praising their accomplishments, emphasise their strengths, and encourage them to try new skills to foster success. Never call them fat or tell them to lose weight. Let them know that it's what's inside that matters and that you love them for who they are. Play down your concerns about their weight – or even your own.

Don't put a child on a diet

You shouldn't restrict your child's calorie intake without the advice of a dietitian. Nutritional needs during childhood are high and important nutrients essential to a child's health could be missed out. Instead make healthy changes to the way they eat. (If you think your child is obese, see your GP, who may advise gradual weight loss under the guidance of a dietitian.)

Set a good example

Children are more likely to copy what you do than do what you say. They learn a lot about food and activity by watching their parents. They should see that you exercise and eat a balanced diet. Share mealtimes as often as possible and eat the same foods.

Don't use food as a reward

Rewarding good behaviour with sweets only reinforces the idea that they're a special treat and makes children crave them more. Allow them in moderation, say, on one day of the week and at the end of a meal.

- Nearly 1 in every 10 six-year olds is obese – that's three children in an average Year One class.

- 1 in every seven 15-year olds is obese.

- One in 6 (17%) boys and nearly 1 in four (23.6%) girls aged 7–11 are overweight.

- A child who is overweight by the age of seven has a 60% chance of being overweight when they are 14–16 years old.

- An overweight teenager has a 70% chance of becoming an overweight adult.

Children's waistlines have expanded by two clothing sizes (4 cm or 1½ in), over the past 20 years, research shows. Waist size is an important indicator of increased risk of heart disease in adulthood, say researchers at Easy Leeds Primary Care Trust.

Don't ban any foods

Allow all foods but explain that certain ones should be eaten only occasionally or kept as special treats. Banning a food increases children's desire for it and makes it more likely that they'll eat it in secret.

Provide healthy snacks

Instead of biscuits, crisps and chocolate make sure there are healthier alternatives to hand at home. Fresh fruit, low fat yoghurt, wholemeal toast, and wholegrain breakfast cereals are good choices (see the box, 'Healthy Snacks'). Keep them in a place where your child can easily get them, for example, a fruit bowl on the table, yoghurts at the front of the fridge.

The average child spends almost 5 hours a day glued to a screen – 2 hours and 5 minutes on the computer and 2 hours and 40 minutes watching television.

WHAT'S A PORTION?

- Pasta or rice – the size of a child's palm
- A baked potato – the size of a child's fist
- Meat, poultry or fish – the size of a deck of cards
- Cheese – 4 dice
- Fruit – the size of a tennis ball
- Vegetables – the amount a child can hold in their hand

IS YOUR CHILD STRESSED?

Stressed children snack more, eat more fatty food, skip breakfast more often and eat fewer fruits and vegetables, say British researchers. A study of over 4,000 London schoolchildren aged 11–12 found that the higher the stress levels, the worse a child's diet becomes.

Get them moving

Look for ways to incorporate activity into everything you do, and make this as much fun as possible. Walk or cycle with your children to and from school. Try to increase the amount of exercise you do together as a family – swimming, playing football, a family walk or bike ride.

Get tough on telly!

Plan exactly what your children will watch on television and agree on a defined time period. Once the programmes have finished, switch off the television, no matter how much they protest. Don't put a TV in your child's bedroom.

77% of 8–14-year olds have a television in their bedroom and psychologists say this distracts children from more active hobbies. Keep your child busy with other activities so he or she won't have much time left for sitting in front of the television.

> **Tip** *A third of all new cases of obesity could be prevented by taking a half-hour walk every day.*

TV TROUBLE

An American study of 6–11-year olds found that those who watched more than five hours of TV a day were more than four times as likely to be overweight as those who watched two hours or less a day.

Researchers have shown that children burn fewer calories watching television than if they were reading or drawing a picture! TV watching induces an almost trance-like state in children, reducing their energy output to a bare minimum.

Watching TV for an extra two hours a day increases the chances of obesity by 25 per cent.

Balance activity and viewing time

Let the number of hours of exercise your children take equal the number of hours of television they're allowed to watch. If they've done an hour's physical activity during the day, you could allocate an hour's television watching.

Don't snack and view

Discourage your children from eating meals or unhealthy snacks while watching television. Because their mind will be on the television and not on the food, they won't notice when they're full up or no longer hungry.

Make exercise fun

Encourage children to pick activities they enjoy – having fun is the key to exercising for life. Provide plenty of play equipment at home – hoppers, balls, trampolines, basketball rings, scooters, bikes and skipping ropes. Introduce them to the wide range of sports available – football, informal racket games, gymnastics, dance lessons, trampolining and swimming. For older children, athletics, roller-skating, hockey, tennis, badminton, netball, jogging, sailing are also great fun.

'IT'S IN THE GENES, ISN'T IT?'

Just as children inherit blue eyes or brown hair, they can inherit a body type that has a greater tendency to put on weight. But – and this is a big but – even if children have inherited a tendency to gain fat, being overweight is by no means inevitable. With a positive attitude, good eating habits and regular activity, they can maintain a sensible weight.

Eat and Stay Slim: Healthy rules for your child (and the rest of the family)

- Follow the one-third rule – vegetables should fill at least one third of the plate. This will help satisfy your child's hunger as well as provide protective nutrients.
- Aim for five portions of fruit and vegetables a day.
- Always eat food sitting at a table – eating in front of the TV or on the run makes you consume more because you don't concentrate fully.
- Give them fruit to take to school for break times – such as apples, satsumas and grapes.

■ Don't ditch dairy products in a bid to save calories: switch to low-fat or skimmed versions. They contain just as much calcium.

■ Offer brown rather than white carbohydrates – wholegrain bread, bran cereals and wholewheat pasta are rich in fibre, which makes your child feel fuller. Switch gradually, though, to avoid stomach upsets.

■ Don't ban chocolate – for treats, offer a fun-sized chocolate bar.

■ Have soup made with lots of veggies more often – it's filling, low in calories, and nutritious. Your children can help make it, or you can buy ready-made fresh versions.

■ Make chips healthier by thickly slicing potatoes and baking them in the oven, tossed in a little olive oil (see Oven Potato Wedges below, page 36)

■ Include fruit for desserts – fresh fruit, stewed apples or pears with custard, baked apples, and fruit crumble.

■ Encourage your child to eat slowly and enjoy every mouthful. Teach by example.

LET THEM EAT FRUIT . . . AND OTHER HEALTHY SNACKS

■ Fresh fruit, e.g. apple slices, satsumas, clementines, grapes, strawberries

■ Wholemeal toast with Marmite

■ Grilled tomatoes on wholemeal toast

■ Low-fat yoghurt

■ Low-fat milk

■ Nuts, e.g. cashews, peanuts, almonds, brazils

■ Wholegrain breakfast cereal with milk

■ Plain popcorn

■ Vegetable crudités (carrot, pepper and cucumber sticks)

■ Rice cake with sliced bananas or cottage cheese

FIT FOR LIFE: HOW MUCH EXERCISE SHOULD CHILDREN GET?

6–10-year olds – 60 minutes of moderate intensity activity as part of their lifestyle every day. It doesn't have to be done in one go.

11–15-year olds – 30–60 minutes of moderate to vigorous activity every day as part of their lifestyle. Plus three sessions per week of continuous vigorous activity lasting at least 20 minutes, e.g. jogging, swimming, cycling, dancing or football.

For both age groups, this recommendation can include everyday activities such as walking, unstructured play such as ball games, 'chase', and hide and seek, sports activities, and PE.

- Start the day with porridge – oats keep your child fuller for longer and keep cravings at bay.
- Include baked beans and lentils in meals – they're filling, nutritious and don't cause a rapid rise in blood sugar, which means they provide longer-lasting energy.
- Encourage your child to drink at least 6 glasses of fluid a day. Thirst is sometimes mistaken for hunger.
- Swap squash and sugary drinks for water with a twist of lemon or lime.

Only one in 20 children use their bicycles as a form of transport in Britain as compared to 14 in 20 in Holland.

Four in 10 are now taken to school by car, compared to less than one in 10 in 1971.

Q&A

Question: How can I avoid mealtimes becoming a battleground?

Answer: Conflicts over food are very common. But you can keep mealtimes as stress-free as possible. Don't comment on how much your child eats. Avoid discussing your child's weight or eating habits at the table. Involve him or her in planning the meal, and, if they wish, preparing and serving the meal too. For example, ask them which vegetables they would prefer ('shall we have cauliflower or broccoli?'), provide a guided choice ('would you prefer minestrone or tomato soup?'; 'would you like baked beans or tuna and sweetcorn with your jacket potato?').

Q&A

Question: What can I do when my child insists on unhealthy snacks?

Answer: The solution is not to have unhealthy snacks in the house. Buy only the kind of food you want your child to eat. It's much harder for a child to fight over a food if it's not there. The trick is to keep treat foods as just that – 'treats' – and buy them only on special occasions.

OVEN POTATO WEDGES

These are a real treat for children. They're healthier than chips as they're lower in fat and, with the skins left on, they retain much of their vitamin C.

Makes 4 servings

- 4 medium potatoes, scrubbed (adjust the quantity according to your children's appetite)
- 4 tsp (20 ml) sunflower or olive oil
- Optional: garlic powder; Parmesan cheese; chilli powder

1 Pre-heat the oven to 200 °C/400 °F/Gas mark 6.

2 Cut each potato lengthways, then cut each half into 6 wedges.

3 Place in a baking tin and turn in the oil until each piece is lightly coated.

4 Bake for 35–40 minutes turning occasionally until the potatoes are soft inside and golden brown on the outside.

5 Sprinkle on one of the optional ingredients 5 minutes before the end of cooking.

Q&A

Question: My child has a big appetite – should I restrict the amount she eats?

Answer: At mealtimes, let her fill up with nutritious foods that contain lots of fibre and water – vegetable dishes, salads, jacket potatoes, wholemeal pasta, fresh fruit and baked apples. If your child is still hungry after the meal, offer her more food, but only the healthy kind – fresh fruit, vegetables, and yoghurt, for example. Resist giving in to demands for unhealthy snacks. Contrary to popular belief, sugary and salty snacks don't fill children up or satisfy their appetite – they can even have the opposite effect, stimulating their taste buds to want more and increasing their thirst for more sugary drinks. It takes time for a child – or indeed an adult – to get used to eating different types and amounts of food.

Summary

- Build your children's self-esteem and make them feel valued – they'll be more likely to make healthier food and activity choices.

- Don't put your child on a diet – instead talk about 'healthy eating'.

- Teach by example – they should see that you exercise and eat a balanced diet.

- Don't ban any food – it'll only increase your child's desire for it.

- Get them moving – encourage active interests, walk or cycle with your children to and from school and exercise together as a family.

Q&A

Question: How can my overweight child eat healthily when the rest of the family want unhealthy foods?

Answer: It's important not to serve your overweight child anything different from the rest of the family. Create healthy habits for everyone. Eliminate unhealthy foods from your household – remove the temptation for the whole family.

tricky little customers

Easy ways to feed fussy eaters

It can be frustrating trying to feed children who refuse to eat proper meals. You worry about them not getting enough calories, becoming malnourished and, as a result, more vulnerable to illness and infection.

- The first thing to remember is that children don't voluntarily starve themselves: they're programmed for survival! As long as there's food available, children will make sure they get enough.

- Secondly, some children are very good at using food to wind up their parents. The more firmly they refuse to finish their plate at mealtimes, the more attention they get. They know that refusing food results in attention.

Young children

Most children go through phases of fussy eating. From as early as their second year, they start to get clear opinions about what they will and won't eat, loving a certain food one day and disliking it the next.

They quickly realise that food is one area where they have control. Refusing a particular food is a way of asserting their independence and gaining attention. The more firmly they reject a particular food, the more attention they get and a vicious circle is soon established. Mealtimes then present the perfect opportunity to test the boundaries.

Older children

Fussy eating isn't just confined to the toddler years. Faddy eating habits often persist for many years – and children don't always just 'grow out of them'. The earlier you tackle the issue, the better. With older children it just takes more perseverance.

Happy Eaters: Making mealtimes easier

Children need to be trained to eat proper meals and nutritious food. You don't have to insist that they clear their plate but you need to set your own rules. A clear strategy will help to persuade your child that food is enjoyable and fun. Ultimately, it will help your child to develop greater confidence around food.

Tips for Tots: Try these solutions for fussy eaters

Get them in the kitchen

Encourage your children to help with the shopping and preparing meals. This will increase their interest in the food, and they'll be more likely to eat the meal if they've been involved in making it.

Q&A

Question: How can I be sure that my daughter isn't starving herself when she eats so little at mealtimes?

Answer: She may be eating more than you think. Does she have snacks between meals or lots of drinks? These can amount to a large proportion of a child's daily food intake. When children consistently refuse meals, many parents are only too pleased for their child to eat something (even if it's a biscuit) rather than nothing. So it's tempting to give in to demands for snacks.

Snacks aren't necessarily a bad thing, provided they supply nutrients in proportion to their energy content. But if your daughter is filling up on biscuits, soft drinks and crisps she won't be getting the vitamins, minerals and fibre she needs. She'll be satisfying her hunger with 'empty' calories and have little appetite left for nutritious food. Follow the advice below on how to encourage proper meals.

Be a good role model

Children learn by example so let them see that you enjoy eating healthy meals. They're more likely to eat foods that they've seen you eat, too. Have meals together whenever possible – ideally once a day, otherwise at least once a week – and show them you enjoy trying new tastes. Serve your children the same food as everyone else.

Build up their appetite

Ensure they've taken plenty of fresh air and exercise; they do wonders for the appetite. It's amazing how less fussy children become if they are really hungry!

Let children serve themselves

Put the food in dishes in the centre of the table so everyone can serve himself or herself. By the age of four most children can judge how much they can eat. You'll also be helping them become more socially aware and independent, allowing them to make their own choices and take responsibility for their actions. My youngest daughter used to refuse bread with margarine. Once I put the bread and margarine out separately on the table, she helped herself to the margarine, spreading on the amount she wanted! Since then, she eats bread with margarine with the rest of the family.

Q&A

Question: What should I do when my fussy eater absolutely insists on snacks between meals?

Answer: Give your child no more than two snacks a day – the first between breakfast and lunch and the second between lunch and tea. There should be no extra snacks if he refuses his meal. Suitable snacks could be fresh fruit (such as sliced apples, bananas, grapes or kiwi fruit), cheese, wholemeal crackers, small wholemeal sandwiches or a carton of yoghurt. No matter how much they protest or request unhealthy snacks, stand firm and don't give them any other food. It will be tough at first – no parent wants to 'starve' their child – but after a week or so they'll soon get the message that the best thing to do at mealtimes is to eat.

Think small

Even if the portion seems ridiculously tiny to you, it's better that your child eats a small amount of everything than nothing at all. A big pile of food on the plate can be off-putting for young children. As a rule of thumb, the younger the child, the smaller the pieces of food – try tiny broccoli florets, small squares of toast, super-thin apple slices.

Keep mealtimes happy

Meals should be enjoyable. Don't discuss eating behaviour, negative food or family issues at mealtimes. Try to achieve a relaxed atmosphere – keep conversation light and fun.

Play with food

You can encourage fussy eaters, especially younger children, to eat good food by presenting it imaginatively. Arrange food in simple shapes, say a circle, a star, a face or a train, or try playing games – such as the train (broccoli) going into the tunnel (mouth)!

Don't get cross

If your child refuses the meal or certain foods, keep your temper. Explain that you expect them to try it and don't offer an alternative. You need to be patient but persistent – not easy, I know, especially when you've spent time preparing a meal. Refusing food loses its appeal if you don't react. (This approach has stretched my patience to the limit, but at the age of six, my youngest daughter now understands that the best thing to do at mealtimes is to eat!)

Don't force feed

You can't make a child eat – he or she will react to your concern and will be even less likely to eat the food. Most adults have bad memories of being made to eat a particular food as a child – remember school dinners? – and then hating it ever since!

Don't bargain with food

It's tempting to say – 'no pudding unless you've eaten your vegetables'. But never promise children a favourite food or dessert *only when* they've finished their main course – this will only reinforce the dislike of the refused food and make the other food seem more special. It's reasonable to expect them to try everything, so you could ask them to have, say, two sprouts, as a compromise. This will seem less daunting.

Keep trying!

If a food is rejected, it doesn't mean they'll never eat it. Children's tastes do change over time. Keep re-introducing those foods they reject, say once a fortnight or once a month, and don't make a fuss. It can take up to 8–10 attempts to get a child to eat a new food. Don't reinforce their dislike of a particular food by telling everyone else that your child won't eat, say, tomatoes, or whatever. He'll be even less likely to try it again.

Give them options

Encourage children to select their own food but from within a limited choice, e.g. 'would you like beans or peas with that?' rather than 'would you like vegetables?'

Set a time limit

If they refuse to eat the meal within, say, 30 minutes, remove it without fuss and don't offer any other food until next mealtime. Be consistent and remember that they won't become malnourished straight away.

Be strict with snacks

If they don't eat their meal, don't let them fill up on snacks later. Eating between meals will simply take away their appetites for more nutritious foods at mealtimes, and perpetuate their taste for those salty, sugary processed foods (see Q&A on page 41: *What should I do when my fussy eater absolutely insists on snacks between meals?*). If they're genuinely hungry, offer only nutritious food – such as fruit, cheese, yoghurt or nuts.

Eating on the move

It's all too easy to get into the habit of feeding your children on the go – in the car or on other transport – or in front of the television. The problem is children won't learn how to eat proper meals and will miss out on the social benefits of eating together. And it'll be harder to break the habit later on, too. Try to organise the family routine so that children eat at the table most of the time.

Summary

- Try to worry less – children won't voluntarily starve themselves.
- Remember, fussy eaters use food as a way of controlling their surroundings, asserting their independence and gaining attention.
- It's essential to have a clear strategy at mealtimes.
- Involve children with menu planning, shopping and the meal preparation whenever possible.
- Set a good example and try to eat together regularly.
- Keep mealtimes happy and avoid confrontations over food.
- Don't get cross or force your children to eat something they dislike.
- Don't bargain with food.
- Children's tastes change over time – keep re-introducing foods.
- Don't allow snacks later if they don't eat their meal.

5 'mum, can I have . . . ?'

How to survive shopping with the children

Supermarket shopping with kids in tow can be fraught with problems. Manufacturers know that children are attracted by bright, fun packaging, cartoon characters and on-pack promotions rather than what's inside. These are all successful marketing ploys to get children to persuade their parents to buy what they want. And the products that appeal most to children are invariably packed with fat, sugar, salt or artificial additives. It's vital to develop a clear strategy to combat pester power when food shopping. Otherwise it can quickly turn into a battle of wills.

Survival tactics

Make a shopping list

And then buy only what's on the list! Having already made your shopping decisions at home, your children will have less time to become distracted by packaging and you have the perfect excuse: 'it's not on the list this week.'

You're in charge!

Remember your children can't actually make you buy anything: you have to decide to buy it! If your children pester you, don't be drawn into an argument. Explain calmly why you won't buy the product (see below) and stand firm. It's not easy, but if you're consistent each time you go shopping, the message will get through.

Avoid tired and hungry moments

Try to schedule shopping when neither you nor the children are vulnerable. They'll be less likely to pester – and you'll be less likely to give in – if you can avoid shopping straight after school, in the evening or just before a meal.

Skip the 'danger' zones

Steer a route through the supermarket avoiding the aisles with the sweets, crisps and fizzy drinks. Where there's less temptation . . .

Check labels

To judge the quality of the food you buy for your children, look at the nutrition information panel on food packages. The Food Standards Agency has issued the guidelines in the box opposite:

	A LOT PER 100 G	A LITTLE PER 100 G
Sugars	10 g	2 g
Total fat	20 g	3 g
Saturated fat	5 g	1 g
Fibre	3 g	0.5 g
Sodium	0.5 g	0.1 g
Salt	1.25 g	0.25 g

Seek out the sugar

Sugar can be hard to spot in children's food as it's called so many different things. Check labels for names such as sucrose, glucose syrup, invert sugar syrup, fructose, dextrose, maltodextrin, fruit syrup and glucose. They're all forms of sugar and all can be harmful to teeth.

Look for other ingredients that can be used to add sweetness – fruit juice, concentrated fruit juice, honey, golden syrup and sweetened condensed milk. They can still damage teeth.

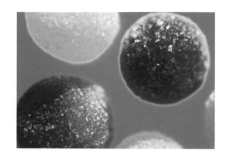

RECOGNISE THE TRICKS OF THE TRADE THAT MAKE PRODUCTS ATTRACTIVE TO CHILDREN

Cartoon characters on food packages are designed to grab children's attention and make you buy the product. But many of these types of products are unhealthy and consist of low-quality ingredients.

What you can do: Look at the ingredients and nutrition label and explain to your children what's wrong with the contents – 'too much sugar or salt' for example. With older children, encourage them to try and find out for themselves – they'll enjoy the challenge – and let them come to their own (and, hopefully, the right) conclusions.

Be strict about on-pack promotions – collectable free gifts or cheap offers for toys and gadgets – will appeal to children.

What you can do: Look carefully at what's in the product before you agree to buy it. If it's a product you'd rather not buy, stand firm and steer your children towards healthier choices.

By encouraging token collection for school books, computer equipment, and membership to clubs, or providing interactive websites, manufacturers encourage brand loyalty. This is fine if it's a healthy product, otherwise this ploy pressurises you to buy products you wouldn't otherwise want for your children.

What you can do: Check whether the number of tokens required is realistic – how many products would you need to buy to earn enough tokens? – and whether they really do offer good value for money.

Children love foods that come in novelty shapes, textures and sizes – anything that makes food easy and fun to eat. Great if it's a healthy product – such as fun-sized cheese portions or squeezy yoghurt pots – but many novelty products are high in sugar, fat or salt (as well as being expensive).

What you can do: Save money by making your own healthy novelty food. Chop vegetables or potatoes into fun shapes, cut small cubes of cheese, serve food in fun dishes, and place healthy snacks like nuts in tiny pots.

Get wise to hydrogenated fat

This processed fat contains trans fats (or trans fatty acids), which have no nutritional benefits. They increase blood levels of LDL ('bad') cholesterol and risk of heart disease. There is no safe limit, says the US Institute of Medicine, while the UK Food Standards Agency recommends you keep your intake to a minimum. Trans fats aren't labelled on packaging; instead look out for hydrogenated or partially hydrogenated fats. Cut down on these:

- **Spreads** made with hydrogenated oils. Expect around 2.8 g/per tablespoon in hard margarine; 0.6 g/per tablespoon in soft (spreadable) margarine. A good alternative is olive oil spread.

- **Fast food**. Most is fried in partially hydrogenated oil – expect up to 14 g in a medium portion of takeaway chips.

- **Cakes and biscuits**. More hydrogenated fat and shortening (high in trans fats) are used in these than any other food – a doughnut contains around 5 g trans fat, a sandwich biscuit as much as 1.9 g. Opt for biscuits made with butter, instead.

- **Crisps and snacks**. Those fried in hydrogenated fat can contain up to 3.2 g per packet.

- **Chocolate bars**. The vegetable fat on the label means hydrogenated fat.

Q&A

Question: Is it better to buy children's foods that have added vitamins?

Answer: By adding extra vitamins to a basically unhealthy product, such as a sugary drink, a sugary processed cereal or a packet of sweets, manufacturers know that parents are more likely to buy it. But this doesn't turn an inherently unhealthy product into a good one. Vitamin-enriched sweets or biscuits are still high in sugar and bad for children's teeth.

If you wouldn't have bought the product without vitamins, don't buy it now.

Spot the additives

Additives are supposed to be safe in theory. But they may provoke an allergic reaction in some children. They're present in up to three-quarters of children's food, according to a survey by Organix. As a result, children could end up eating huge amounts of additives by the time they reach their teens. Sweets, savoury snacks, desserts and snack bars are the worst offenders.

A government-funded study at the UK's Asthma and Allergy Research Centre found that certain food colours and preservatives cause hyperactive behaviour in as many as one in four young children. They recommended that **all** children (not only hyperactive children) would benefit from the removal of artificial food colourings from their diet. These are the additives to look out for on food labels:

Colours
Tartrazine (E102)
Sunset Yellow (E110)
Carmoisine (E122)
Ponceau 4R (E124)

Preservative
Sodium Benzoate (E211)

Q&A

Question: How can I stop my children nagging me for sweets and chocolates displayed at the checkout?

Answer: It is infuriating that many supermarkets display sweets and snacks at their checkouts, on aisle ends or in dump-bins near the tills. Such tempting displays are deliberately placed to activate pester power and increase sales. Here's what you can do:

- Avoid shops that sell sweets at the checkout. (Asda is committed to substituting confectionery with healthy snacks and fruit and vegetables at its checkouts.)

- Tell supermarkets what you think – write to the manager of the store.

- Join the 'Chuck Sweets off the Checkout!' campaign run by the Parents' Jury of the Food Commission (www.parentsjury.org.uk).

Summary

- Avoid doing the shopping when you and the children are tired or hungry.

- Make a shopping list – and then buy only what's on the list. Remember you're in charge – the children can't make you buy anything you don't want.

- Be sensible. Don't encourage your children to choose which product they want if it's one you'd actually rather they didn't eat at all!

- Recognise the tricks of the trade that make products attractive to children.

- Look at the labels and explain to children what's wrong with the contents.

- Check labels for hidden sugar, hydrogenated fat and artificial additives.

Secrets of a healthy lunchbox

It's a daily challenge. Who doesn't struggle for inspiration on what to put into their child's lunchbox each morning? Who doesn't wonder whether the food they're giving their child for lunch provides enough nutrients? And what parent doesn't suspect that it may come home uneaten anyway?

A successful lunchbox is enjoyable and filling and also provides children with enough energy to sustain them for several hours of work and play. Lunch should supply approximately one third of a child's daily energy needs, as well as one third of their protein, carbohydrate, fibre, vitamin and mineral requirements.

Pack a variety of different foods in your child's lunchbox. Instead of basic sandwiches, try:

■ Pizza slices

■ Pasta, potato or rice salad in a small tub

■ A meat or vegetarian sausage

■ Soup in a flask

■ Tortilla wraps with interesting fillings

■ Slices of rolled up lean meat

■ Cheese dips or pate with vegetable sticks

■ A spring roll or samosa

■ A chicken drumstick or wing.

All of these options provide a good balance of carbohydrate and protein, while reducing salt and additives.

THE PERFECT LUNCHBOX

■ A drink (200–300 ml)

■ At least 1 portion of fresh or dried fruit

■ One portion of salad or vegetables (such as carrot sticks or salad in a sandwich)

■ One carbohydrate food (such as bread, pasta or rice)

■ One dairy food or calcium-rich food (such as cheese, yoghurt, fromage frais or milk)

■ One protein-rich food (such as meat, fish, peanut butter, hummus or egg)

A 2003 SURVEY OF 556 LUNCHBOXES BY THE FOOD STANDARDS AGENCY FOUND:

Nine out of ten children's lunch boxes contain double the recommended daily amount of sugar and nearly half the safe daily intake for salt and saturated fats. The most popular items are white bread sandwiches (found in nearly 9 out of 10 lunchboxes), crisps (found in seven out of ten) and a chocolate bar or cake (found in six out of ten).

Fewer than half of all children have a portion of fruit in their lunchbox.

Drinks

Lunchtime goal? Between 200 and 300 ml each day

A lunchtime drink is important to keep children properly hydrated and avoid flagging energy levels in the afternoon. Even mild dehydration results in headaches, fatigue and poor concentration. Remember, children need 6–8 glasses a day. Drinking plenty of fluid is also important to help their kidneys, brain and digestive system work properly.

KEEPING IT FRESH!

Foods such as yoghurt, fromage frais, milk, milkshake, dips, pate, cooked meat and chicken should be kept cool so it's a good idea to use an insulated lunchbox. Alternatively, slip a small ice-pack into your child's lunchbox to keep the contents fresh. Or put lots of ice cubes into your child's drinks bottle and place this inside. The ice will have melted by lunchtime but it will keep the food cool.

BEST CHOICES

- Water
- Milk or milkshake (keep chilled in a thermos) (see recipes pages 129 and 132)
- Fruit juice (ideally diluted at least one part juice, one part water)
- Fruit smoothie (see recipes pages 130–2)
- Yoghurt drink (ideally probiotic varieties)
- Organic fruit cordial (diluted one part cordial ten parts water)

LESS SUITABLE

- Fizzy drinks (contain too much sugar and too many artificial additives).
- Fruit drinks, squash and soft drinks (contain too much sugar and too many artificial additives).

Lunchbox Treats

Fruit and vegetables

Lunchtime goal: 1 portion of fruit and 1 portion of vegetables or salad

- Fruit and vegetables are much more appealing if they're quick and easy to eat. Give small fruit (say, little apples or satsumas, grapes or strawberries) or cut bigger fruits into bite-sized pieces.

- Small ring-pull tins of fruit in juice and small cartons of fruit purée – from supermarkets – are also tasty.

- Small boxes and bags of dried fruit are nutritious and fun to eat. My daughters adore dried tropical fruit and apricots (rich in beta-carotene and iron). But dried fruit can stick to the teeth, so encourage your children to follow with an apple and/or a piece of cheese (this reduces the acidity and helps re-mineralise the tooth enamel).

- Try fruit smoothies – they make a good alternative to whole fruit.

- Wrap carrot, pepper, cherry tomatoes, celery sticks or cucumber sticks in cling film or put in a small plastic pot. Serve with a small pot of hummus, salad cream or a cheesy dip. Add salad vegetables (say, salad leaves, tomatoes or cucumber) to sandwiches.

BEST VEGETABLE CHOICES

- Sticks of carrots, cucumber, peppers
- Baby sweetcorn
- Tomato, cucumber, lettuce or cress in a sandwich filling
- Cherry tomatoes

BEST FRUIT CHOICES

- Apples, pears
- Satsumas, clementines, mandarins
- Bananas, Grapes, cherries
- Kiwi fruit (children can cut them in half and scoop out the flesh with a spoon)
- Small container of strawberries, blueberries or raspberries
- Peaches, nectarines
- Small boxes of raisins
- Small bags of apricots, mango, pineapple, raisins, dried fruit
- Ring-pull cans or long-life cartons of fruit in juice
- Cartons and pots of fruit purée

Sandwiches

- Vary the type of bread you use for sandwiches. Try mini pittas, wraps (fill them then cut into lengths that small hands can cope with), bagels, small rolls or English muffins.

- Use wholemeal or brown bread most of the time – it contains three times as much fibre and more iron and B vitamins. White bread with added fibre contains only a little more fibre than ordinary white.

- Try using different types of bread – walnut bread, raisin or fruit bread, seeded bread or cheese and herb bread.

Sandwich fillings

Ideally, fillings should include a **protein-rich food** – cheese, chicken, ham, turkey, peanut butter, tuna or hummus – and a salad vegetable (say, cucumber or tomato).

Avoid sugary fillings such as jam or chocolate-spread – they provide extra calories (in the form of sugar) but very few essential nutrients. Keep for occasional treats.

Stuck for ideas? Try the following nutritious fillings:

- **Ham and tomato** – Lay three or four thin slices of tomato over a slice of lean ham.

- **Peanut butter with cucumber** – Spread each slice of bread with peanut butter instead of your usual spread then lay several cucumber slices on top.

- **Marmite and cheese** – Spread one slice of bread with Marmite (yeast extract) and cover with grated cheese.

- **Soft cheese with tuna and lettuce** – Mix one tablespoon of soft cheese with an equal amount of tuna. Add shredded lettuce.

- **Mozzarella and tomato** – Lay thin slices of mozzarella on one side of the bread and cover with thin tomato slices.

- **Hardboiled egg mixed with mayonnaise and cress** – Mash one hard-boiled egg roughly with 2 teaspoons of mayonnaise. Stir in a little cress.

- **Banana and honey** – Roughly mash half a banana with a one teaspoon of lemon juice (to stop discolouration) and half a teaspoon of honey.

- **Turkey slices with cranberry sauce** – Chop one or two slices of roast turkey with a teaspoon of cranberry sauce.

MINI CHEESE AND VEGETABLE TARTLETTES

- ½ pack (200 g) ready-rolled shortcrust pastry
- 60 g (2 oz) Cheddar cheese
- 3 eggs
- 125 ml (4 fl oz) milk
- 2 tbsp sweetcorn
- 2 tbsp chopped red peppers
- 1 tomato, chopped

1 Pre-heat the oven to 200 °C/ 400 °F/Gas mark 6.

2 Butter or oil 6 holes of a deep muffin tin.

3 Place the ready-rolled pastry on a floured surface and cut into 6 rounds using an 8 cm (3") cutter.

4 Lightly press into the 6 muffin holes.

5 Combine the cheese, eggs and milk, and stir in the sweetcorn, peppers and tomato, then spoon into the muffin tin.

6 Bake in the oven for 20 minutes or until risen and golden.

7 Leave to cool for a few minutes before removing from the tin.

Around half of all schoolchildren take a packed lunch to school every day.

- **Avocado and chicken** – Mash half of an avocado with one teaspoon of lemon juice (to stop discolouration). Chop two slices of roast chicken and mix with the avocado.

- **Hummus and grated carrot** – Mix one tablespoon of hummus (ready-made or see recipe on page 58) with one finely grated carrot.

- **Cottage cheese and fruit** – Mix cottage cheese with extra raisins, chopped dried apricots or dried mango.

- **Salmon and cucumber** – Roughly mash one tablespoon of tinned salmon and lay on top of thinly sliced cucumber.

- **Chopped chicken and coleslaw** – Chop two slices of roast chicken and mix with one tablespoon of coleslaw.

BREAD AND OTHER STARCHY FOODS

- Wholemeal, malted grain or wheatgerm bread
- Wholemeal roll
- Mini-pitta bread
- English muffin
- Mini-bagel
- Wrap
- Wholemeal crackers
- Rice crackers/rice cakes
- Pot of potato salad
- Pot of pasta or rice salad
- Slice of pizza

Wraps

Soft flour wraps can be found in most supermarkets and make perfect wrappings for savoury fillings. Place the filling to the side of the centre of the wrap, fold over the unfilled half then roll up. Cut into 2 to 4 pieces to serve. For a lunchbox, wrap in non-stick baking paper.

Try these yummy flavours:

- **Cheese with tomato** – Mix 2 tablespoons of grated cheese with one chopped tomato.

- **Egg and cress** – Roughly chop a hard-boiled or scrambled egg with one tablespoon of salad cream and a little cress.

- **Chicken and lettuce** – Chop 2 cooked chicken slices and mix with 2 teaspoons of mayonnaise and some chopped lettuce.

- **Tuna and cucumber** – Mix 2 tablespoons of tinned tuna with 2 teaspoons of mayonnaise and chopped cucumber.

- **Ham, tomato and cucumber** – Lay 2 slices of lean ham on the wrap and cover with slices of tomatoes and cucumber.

- **Banana** – Toss one sliced banana in 1 teaspoon of lemon juice.

LUNCHABLES

Ready-bought 'lunchable' style products generally contain very high levels of saturated fat and salt and don't provide much fibre or vitamins. Check the label and compare with the guide on page 47. Anything containing more than 1.25 g salt per 100 g is too high. Also check the ingredients for artificial preservatives, sweeteners, colours and flavourings.

Calcium-rich foods

Lunchbox goal: one dairy or soya serving

■ Good dairy foods for lunches include cheese, yoghurt, fromage frais, milk or milkshake; or try a soya alternative – soya milk, soya 'yoghurt' or dessert. They all provide calcium, which is important for building healthy bones. Sardines and nuts (especially almonds) are another source of calcium.

■ Try to buy yoghurt and fromage frais that don't contain artificial sweeteners, colours, and flavourings. In general organic varieties are best as they don't contain additives.

■ Yoghurt pouches and tubes of fromage frais are great for eating on the go.

HUMMUS

This dip is an excellent source of fibre, protein and iron. Use as a filling for sandwiches or for dipping raw vegetables, such as carrot, pepper and cucumber sticks.

Makes 4 servings

- 400 g (14 oz) tinned chickpeas
- 2 garlic cloves, crushed
- 2 tbsp (30 ml) extra virgin olive oil
- 120 ml (4 fl oz) tahini (sesame seed paste)
- Juice of 1 lemon
- 2–4 tbsp (30–60 ml) water
- A little low-sodium salt and freshly ground black pepper
- Pinch of paprika or cayenne pepper

1 Drain and rinse the chickpeas. Put them in a food processor or blender with the remaining ingredients, apart from the paprika. Process to a smooth paste. Add extra water if necessary to give the desired consistency.

2 Adjust the seasoning to taste.

3 Spoon into a serving dish. Pour over a little olive oil and sprinkle with cayenne or paprika.

4 Chill in the fridge for at least 2 hours before serving.

PROTEIN-RICH AND CALCIUM-RICH FOODS FOR LUNCHBOXES

■ Cheese in a sandwich

■ Individual cheese portion

■ Chicken drumsticks

■ Low-fat sausages/vegetarian sausages

■ Carton, pouch or tube of yoghurt*

■ Carton, pouch or tube of fromage frais

■ Carton or bottle of milk*

■ Milkshake*

■ Yoghurt drink*

■ Carton of custard

■ Pilchards in a sandwich

■ Nuts (say, mixed with dried fruit or in a salad)

* Dairy or soya equivalent

Extras

- Little extras make a varied lunch – try to provide healthy items most of the time (see box opposite).

- Chocolate-coated bars, cakes, crisps and biscuits shouldn't be included every day – they're loaded with unhealthy fats and sugar and are especially harmful to teeth if they're the last thing to be eaten.

- If children must have sugary foods, encourage them to eat a piece of fruit and a small piece of cheese afterwards – this helps counteract some of the damaging effects of sugar.

Q&A

Question: What should I do when my daughter asks for crisps and biscuits in her lunchbox so she can eat the same things as her friends?
Answer: No child likes to be different. But you don't have to surrender your principles. You can compromise by allowing crisps – ideally the lower salt kind – one day of the week.

As for other favourite snacks, why not make your own biscuits (see Wholemeal raisin biscuits, page 63) or muffins (see Fruit muffins, page 61)? When my eldest daughter first took a kiwi fruit with a small knife and spoon to school, her friends were so intrigued, they requested one too! Let your child choose her own healthy treats – small bags of dried fruit, small ring-pull tins of fruit, novelty cheeses or yoghurt tubes.

Q&A

Question: What can I put in my child'd lunchbox instead of chocolate for a treat?
Answer: A chocolate treat is often a way of saying 'I'm thinking about you and I care for you'. But you can say this in other ways. Why not pop in a little note that says 'I love you', or a picture of a favourite cartoon character, animal or joke? My daughters eagerly anticipate the surprise notes and pictures in their lunchboxes, show their friends and save them at home in a little folder. At least they have fond, lasting reminders of lunchbox treats that don't damage teeth.

HEALTHIER EXTRAS

- Small packet of dried fruit (e.g. raisins, mango, apricots, dates, pineapple)
- A few nuts
- A few grapes
- Scone
- Fruit bun or teacake
- Mini-pancake
- Cereal bar (without hydrogenated fat)
- Breadsticks
- Rice crackers or rice cakes
- Plain popcorn
- Crisps that come with a separate packet of salt – remove the salt or add only half
- Homemade muffins, biscuits and fruit loaves (see recipes pp 123–7)
- Small bags of dried fruit

FRUIT MUFFINS

These are made with wholemeal flour; it contains fibre, iron and vitamins. Raisins also provide valuable fibre as well as lots of antioxidants.

Makes 12 muffins

- 125 g (4 oz) white self-raising flour
- 125 g (4 oz) wholemeal self-raising flour
- Pinch of salt
- 40 g (1½ oz) soft brown sugar
- 2 tbsp (30 ml) rapeseed oil
- 1 size 3 egg
- 200 ml (7 fl oz) milk
- 85 g (3 oz) raisins or sultanas

1 Pre-heat the oven to 220 °C/425 °F/Gas mark 7.

2 Mix the flours and salt together in a bowl.

3 Add the sugar, oil, egg and milk. Mix well.

4 Stir in the dried fruit.

5 Spoon into non-stick muffin tins and bake for 15–20 minutes until golden brown.

BANANA MUFFINS

These tasty banana muffins are made with healthy rapeseed oil, which is rich in essential fats (including omega-3 fats).

Makes 12 muffins

- 2 large ripe bananas, mashed
- 85 g (3 oz) soft brown sugar
- 4 tbsp (60 ml) rapeseed oil
- 1 size 3 egg
- 125 ml (4 fl oz) milk
- 200 g (7 oz) self-raising flour
- Pinch of salt
- ½ tsp (2.5 ml) nutmeg, grated

1 Preheat the oven to 190 °C/375 °F/Gas mark 5.

2 In a bowl, mix together the bananas, sugar and oil.

3 Beat in the egg and milk.

4 Fold in the flour, salt and nutmeg.

5 Spoon into non-stick muffin tins and bake for 15–20 minutes.

DELICIOUSLY CLEVER: ONE MONTH OF LUNCHBOXES

	WEEK 1	WEEK 2	WEEK 3	WEEK 4
Monday	Wholemeal chicken and tomato sandwich 1 pot of fruit yoghurt 6–7 carrot sticks 1 satsuma Apple juice (ideally, diluted 50/50 with water).	Mini-bagel filled with soft cheese and sliced banana 1 small bunch of grapes 1 pot of fromage frais Bottle of water	Wholemeal roll filled with tuna, sweetcorn and mayonnaise 6–7 carrot sticks Individual cheese portion Small bag of dried fruit (e.g. mango, pineapple) Bottle of water	Rice salad with cooked chicken, peas and sweetcorn 1 pear Milkshake
Tuesday	Flask of vegetable soup Wholemeal roll and butter Small bag of dried fruit Individual cheese portion Orange juice (ideally, diluted 50/50 with water)	Mini tartlette (see recipe page 55) 6–7 carrot sticks 1 pot of fromage frais Fruit Smoothie	4 wholemeal crackers Hummus dip Vegetable sticks, say cucumber, carrots or celery Handful of grapes 1 pot of fruit yoghurt Bottle of water	Flask of tomato soup 1 wholemeal cheese roll 1 satsuma 1 wholemeal raisin biscuit (see recipe page 63) Bottle of water
Wednesday	Slice of homemade pizza 4–5 strips of peppers or 4–5 cherry tomatoes 1 apple 1 yoghurt drink	Cooked tofu sausage or quorn sausage (wrapped in foil) Wholemeal Marmite sandwich Small handful of nuts in a pot (e.g. cashews or peanuts) 1 clementine Bottle of water	1 cooked chicken drumstick (wrapped in foil) Small Marmite sandwich 1 plum Apple juice (ideally, diluted 50/50 with water)	Cheese dip or pate Carrot, pepper and cucumber sticks A few breadsticks 1 pear Yoghurt drink
Thursday	Pasta salad with tuna, peppers and mushrooms 1 pot fruit yoghurt 1 small bag of dried apricots Apple juice (ideally, diluted 50/50 with water)	Mini wholemeal pitta filled with tinned salmon and salad Handful of cherries Mini box of raisins Yoghurt drink	1 bagel with soft cheese and sliced cucumber 4 cherry tomatoes 1 ring-pull can of fruit in juice Bottle of water	Wholemeal roll filled with chicken and coleslaw Cereal bar (see recipe page 65) 1 apple Milkshake
Friday	Tortilla wrap filled with cooked turkey and coleslaw 1 small ring-pull tin of fruit in juice 1 carton of milk	Mixed bean salad (in a tub) 1 peach 1 carton of custard Orange juice (ideally, diluted 50/50 with water)	Wrap filled with ham, tomato and cucumber slices 1 banana Yoghurt drink	Wholemeal peanut butter and cucumber roll Individual cheese portion Strawberries (in a small tub) 1 pot of fromage frais Bottle of water

WHOLEMEAL RAISIN BISCUITS

These biscuits are far healthier than bought ones. They're lower in sugar and higher in fibre.

Makes 20 biscuits

- 225 g (8 oz) wholemeal plain flour
- 40 g (1½ oz) brown sugar
- 85 g (3 oz) raisins
- 2 tbsp (30 ml) rapeseed oil
- 1 size 3 egg
- 4 tbsp (60 ml) milk

1 Pre-heat the oven to 180 °C/350 °F/Gas mark 4.

2 Combine the flour, sugar and raisins in a bowl.

3 Stir in the oil, egg and milk and lightly mix together until you have a stiff dough.

4 Place spoonfuls of the mixture onto a lightly oiled baking tray.

5 Bake for 12–15 minutes until golden brown.

BANANA LOAF

This healthy version of banana cake is made with wholemeal flour, brown sugar and rapeseed oil instead of the usual white flour, white sugar and butter.

Makes 12 slices

- 225 g (8 oz) self-raising wholemeal flour
- 125 g (4 oz) brown sugar
- Pinch of salt
- ½ tsp each of mixed spice and cinnamon
- 2 large ripe bananas
- 175 ml (6 fl oz) orange juice
- 2 size 3 eggs
- 4 tbsp (60 ml) rapeseed oil

1 Pre-heat the oven to 170 °C/325 °F/Gas mark 4.

2 Mix together the flour, sugar, salt and spices in a bowl.

3 Mash the bananas with the orange juice.

4 Combine the mashed banana mixture, eggs and oil with the flour mixture.

5 Spoon into a lightly oiled 2 lb loaf tin.

6 Bake for about 1 hour. Check the cake is done by inserting a skewer or knife into the centre. It should come out clean.

APRICOT BARS

Dried apricots are packed with beta-carotene, a powerful antioxidant that boosts immunity and protects against illness.

Makes 8 bars

- 125 g (4 oz) self-raising white flour
- 60 g (2 oz) sugar
- 125 g (4 oz) dried apricots
- 6 tbsp (90 ml) orange juice
- 2 size 3 eggs
- 125 g (4 oz) sultanas

1 Preheat the oven to 180 °C/350 °F/Gas mark 4.

2 Mix together the flour and sugar in a bowl.

3 Blend together the apricots and juice in a liquidiser or food processor until smooth.

4 Add the apricot purée, eggs and sultanas to the flour & sugar. Mix together.

5 Spoon the mixture into an 18 cm (7 in) square cake tin. Bake for 30–35 minutes until golden brown. Allow to cool. Cut into 8 bars.

Summary

- Make sure the lunchbox you provide is attractive, varied and imaginative.

- Keep it balanced; include a drink, a portion of fresh or dried fruit, a portion of salad or vegetables, some carbohydrate (wholemeal bread, pasta or rice), a dairy or calcium-rich food, and a protein-rich food (meat, cheese, peanut butter).

- Vary the type of bread you use for sandwiches – try seeded bread, mini pittas, tortilla wraps, bagels, or fancy rolls.

- Instead of sandwiches every day, try pizza slices, pasta, potato or rice salad, a sausage, soup in a flask, slices of rolled up lean meat, dips or pate with vegetable sticks, or a chicken drumstick.

- Give fruit in a form that can be easily eaten – small fruits, easy-to-peel varieties or fruit cut into bite-sized pieces.

- The easiest way to include vegetables in a lunchbox is to cut them into manageable pieces (say, carrot sticks), add them to a sandwich filling or mix them with pasta in a salad.

- Instead of sugary foods and crisps, try small packets of dried fruit, a few nuts, grapes, a scone or fruit bun, plain popcorn, or healthier home-made muffins, biscuits and fruit loaves.

- If children occasionally have sugary foods, encourage them to follow with a piece of fruit and a small piece of cheese – this helps counteract some of the damaging effects of sugar.

CEREAL BARS

These highly nutritious bars are made from oats and muesli, which provide lots of fibre, B vitamins and sustained energy. They're lower in fat than shop-bought cereal bars.

Makes 12 bars

- 175 g (6 oz) oats
- 85 g (3 oz) no added sugar muesli
- 150 g (5 oz) dried fruit mixture
- 3 tbsp (45 ml) honey, clear or set
- 2 egg whites
- 175 ml (6 fl oz) apple juice

1 Pre-heat the oven to 180 °C/350 °F/Gas mark 4.

2 Combine the oats, muesli and dried fruit in a bowl.

3 Warm the honey in a small saucepan until it is runny. Add to the bowl.

4 Stir in the remaining ingredients.

5 Press the mixture into a lightly oiled 18 x 28 cm (7 x 11 in) baking tin. Bake for 20–25 minutes until golden.

6 When cool, cut into bars.

7 *fun with food*

Kids in the kitchen

Cooking can be great fun for children. Creating their own dishes gives them a sense of achievement, and can be a superb way to motivate fussy eaters to try new tastes and gain confidence with food. Preparing meals can also be educational; children quickly pick up new skills when they're enjoying themselves – they'll learn about weighing, measuring, mixing, spreading, cutting, organising and following instructions, as well as finding out how ingredients work together.

Try these eight recipes; they're easy enough for older children to make on their own. (Younger children may need help from an adult.)

STRIPY CHEESE ON TOAST

Makes 2 portions
- 2 slices of bread
- 40 g (1½ oz) Cheddar cheese
- 40 g (1½ oz) Red Leicester cheese
- You'll need: a sharp knife, chopping board, grill pan

1 Pre-heat the grill.

2 Toast the bread on both sides in a toaster or under the grill.

3 Slice the cheese into strips about 2 cm (¾ inch) wide and 5 mm (¼ inch) thick.

4 Lay alternating slices of Cheddar and Red Leicester on the toast until the toast is covered.

5 Place the toast on the grill rack and place under the grill for about 1 minute until the cheese has melted and started bubbling.

BREADSTICKS

Makes about 20
- 750 g (1½ lb) strong white flour
- 7 g (1 sachet) easy blend yeast
- 450 ml (¾ pint) warm water
- 1 tsp salt
- 1 tbsp olive oil

You'll need: a large mixing bowl, a wooden spoon, a knife, 2 baking trays, clingfilm, oven gloves

1 Put the flour, yeast, warm water, salt and olive oil into a mixing bowl.

2 Mix them all together using a wooden spoon, then use your hands to bring the mixture together.

3 Sprinkle the worktop with flour and take the mixture out of the bowl. Knead the dough for 10 minutes. It should be smooth and stretchy, not sticky.

4 Cut the dough into about 20 pieces. Roll each out to make a 25 cm (10 inch) long stick.

5 Grease the baking trays. Put the breadsticks spaced apart on to the baking trays. Cover loosely with clingfilm and leave it in a warm place. Leave until it's doubled in size – about 30 minutes.

6 Meanwhile heat the oven to 200 °C/400 °F/Gas mark 6.

7 Remove the clingfilm and bake the breadsticks in the oven for 6–8 minutes until golden.

Tip: You can make different shapes with the bread dough or decorate with beaten egg and sunflower or poppy seeds just before putting in the oven.

VEGETABLE SOUP

Makes 4 servings
- 1 large onion
- 1 red pepper
- 2 large carrots
- 1 potato
- 1 tbsp olive oil
- 2 tsp Swiss vegetable bouillon powder or 1 vegetable stock cube
- 900 ml (1½ pints) water

You'll need: chopping board, vegetable peeler, sharp knife, large saucepan with a lid, wooden spoon

1 On the chopping board, peel then chop the onion.

2 Cut the pepper in half, cut away the white pith and scrape away the seeds. Cut into small squares.

3 Using the vegetable peeler, peel and cut the carrots and potato into small pieces (you may need to ask an adult to help).

4 Put the oil in the saucepan and put over a low heat. Add the onions and cook for 5 minutes, stirring with a wooden spoon, until see-through and soft.

5 Add the rest of the vegetables and stock powder/cube. Pour in the water. Bring the mixture to the boil, cover then turn down the heat and simmer for 30 minutes over a low heat.

6 The soup is ready to serve. If you don't like lumpy soup, use a blender until it's smooth. Let the soup cool before blending (you may need to ask an adult to help you use a blender).

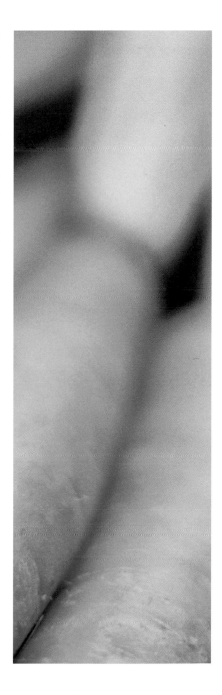

JACKET POTATO WITH TUNA AND CUCUMBER

- 4 potatoes
- 200 g (7 oz) tin tuna
- Half a cucumber
- 4 tbsp mayonnaise

You'll need: vegetable brush, fork, tin opener, small bowl, chopping board, small sharp knife, metal spoon

1 Heat the oven to 200 °C/400 °F/Gas mark 6.

2 Scrub the potatoes with the vegetable brush. Prick the skin with a fork. Bake in the oven for about 1 hour or until the flesh is soft.

3 Meanwhile, open the can of tuna and drain off the liquid. Put the tuna in a bowl and break it roughly with a fork.

4 On the chopping board, cut the cucumber in half lengthways. Cut each half in half lengthways again. Cut each segment into slices about 5 mm (¼ inch) thick.

5 Add the cucumber to the tuna with the mayonnaise. Mix together with the spoon.

6 Remove the potatoes from the oven (ask an adult to help with this). Cut a cross in the top of each potato and gently prise open (again, ask an adult to help). Spoon the tuna and cucumber mixture over the top of the potatoes.

Here are some other toppings for jacket potatoes
- baked beans
- grated cheddar cheese
- crème fraiche
- salsa
- stir-fried vegetables
- chopped chicken or turkey mixed with a little mayonnaise
- hummus
- cottage cheese
- prawns with mayonnaise
- ratatouille
- grilled mushrooms
- chilli (see recipe page 93)
- scrambled egg and tomato
- sweetcorn
- Bolognese sauce (see recipe page 88 and 98)

SULTANA SCONES

Makes 12
- 225 g (8 oz) self-raising flour
- 60 g (2 oz) butter or margarine
- 60 g (2 oz) caster sugar
- 60 g (2 oz) sultanas
- 150 ml (¼ pint) milk

You'll need: mixing bowl, palette knife, baking sheet, rolling pin, 5 cm (2 inch) cutter, oven gloves, wire rack

1 Heat the oven to 230 °C/450 °F/Gas mark 8.

2 Grease a baking sheet with butter or margarine.

3 Put the flour in a mixing bowl. Add the margarine and rub in with your fingertips until the mixture looks like fine breadcrumbs. Stir in the sultanas.

4 Stir in enough milk to form a soft dough, using the palette knife.

5 Sprinkle flour on the work surface and knead the dough lightly for a few moments.

6 Roll out the dough until 2 cm (¾ inch) thick. Cut out rounds with a floured cutter and place on the greased baking sheet.

7 Bake in the oven for 10 minutes until risen and golden. Transfer to a wire rack to cool.

CHOCOLATE CHIP MUFFINS

Makes 12
- 250 g (9 oz) self-raising flour
- 85 g (3 oz) sugar
- 200 ml (7 fl oz) milk
- 1 egg
- ½ tsp (2.5 ml) vanilla extract
- 85 g (3 oz) butter or margarine, melted
- 85 g (3 oz) chocolate chips

You'll need: a muffin tin, 12 paper cases, mixing bowl, wooden spoon, metal spoon

1 Heat the oven to 200 °C/400 °F/Gas mark 6.

2 Line the muffin tin with paper cases.

3 Mix together the flour and sugar in a large bowl.

4 Combine the milk, egg, vanilla extract and melted butter or margarine in a separate bowl.

5 Pour the liquid ingredients into a well in the flour mixture. Mix together.

6 Add the chocolate chips and combine briefly.

7 Spoon the mixture into the muffin tin. Bake for about 15 minutes or until risen and golden.

FRUIT SMOOTHIE

You can use other varieties of fresh fruit or even frozen or tinned fruit. Try making a smoothie with a mango and peach. Or an apple and a banana. Just add fruit juice or milk and yoghurt. You may need to ask an adult to help you use the blender.

Makes 2 glasses

- 6 strawberries
- 1 handful of raspberries
- 1 banana
- 450 ml (¾ pint) milk or orange juice
- 1 tbsp yoghurt

You'll need: a knife, chopping board, smoothie maker, blender or food processor

1 Slice the green tops of the strawberries. Peel the banana and cut into thick slices.

2 Put the fruit into the smoothie maker, blender or food processor.

3 Add the milk or orange juice and the yoghurt.

4 Put the lid on the machine and blend together for about 30 seconds.

5 Pour into 2 glasses.

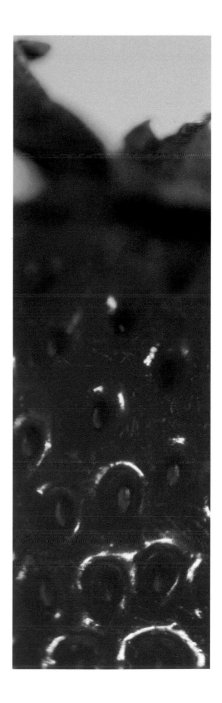

FLAPJACKS

Makes 12

- 125 g (4 oz) butter or margarine
- 125 g (4 oz) sugar
- 125 g (4 oz) golden syrup
- 225 g (8 oz) rolled oats (porridge oats)

You'll need: a 15 cm (6 inch) square baking tin, a 15 cm (6 inch) square of greaseproof paper, a small saucepan, a tablespoon, a teaspoon, a wooden spoon, a mixing bowl, oven gloves.

1 Heat the oven to 160 °C/325 °F/Gas mark 3.

2 Grease a 15 cm (6 inch) square baking tin and line with greaseproof paper.

3 Put the butter or margarine, sugar and syrup in the saucepan. Put the oats in a mixing bowl.

4 Using a wooden spoon, stir the ingredients in the pan over a low heat until just melted. Remove from the heat. Pour onto the oats and mix well.

5 Put the mixture into the tin and press down, levelling off the top with a tablespoon.

6 Bake in the oven for 20 minutes until golden brown around the edges but still soft in the middle.

7 Mark into 12 bars while still hot. Turn out of tin when cool.

good health on a plate

Menu plans for balanced eating

Variety is the key to healthy, balanced eating, so aim to use the following menu plans as a basis for developing your child's daily diet. These menus are in line with the dietary recommendations of the children's food guide pyramid (see p 4) and provide a good balance of carbohydrate, protein, fat, vitamins and minerals.

There are two seven day menu plans for 5–10 year olds and two seven day menu plans for 11–15-year olds, each including a vegetarian eating plan. Judge the portion sizes according to your children's age, activity and appetite. Encourage your children to drink 6–8 glasses of fluid (water, diluted fruit juice, milk) daily, and more during exercise or in hot weather.

SEVEN DAY MENU PLAN FOR 5–10-YEAR OLDS

Monday

Breakfast — Wholegrain cereal with milk
Banana

Lunchbox — Tuna, cucumber and mayonnaise wholemeal sandwich
Small ring-pull can of fruit in juice
Carton of yoghurt
Water

Dinner — Chicken burgers (see recipe page 86)
Oven potato wedges (see recipe page 108)
Baked beans or broccoli
Stewed apples and raisins

Tuesday

Breakfast — Wholemeal toast and peanut butter or Marmite
Fresh fruit
Milk or yoghurt

Lunchbox — Slice of pizza
Raw carrot and cucumber sticks
Small bunch of seedless grapes
Pot of fromage frais
Orange juice

Dinner — Pasta and tuna bake (see recipe page 92)
Sliced tomatoes with a little dressing
Yoghurt and fruit pudding

Wednesday

Breakfast — Porridge made with milk and water
A little honey and raisins

Lunchbox — Pitta bread filled with cold chopped chicken and coleslaw
4–5 dried apricots
Small carton of milk

Dinner — Toad-and-vegetables-in-the-hole (see recipe page 91)
Spring cabbage or broccoli
Fresh fruit

Thursday

Breakfast — Banana smoothie (see recipe page 130)

Lunchbox — Wholemeal roll filled with lean ham and tomato
Piece of fresh fruit
Carton of custard
Water

Dinner — Jacket potato filled with baked beans and grated cheese
or with scrambled egg and tomato
Crunchy apple crumble (see recipe page 118)

SEVEN DAY MENU PLAN FOR 5–10-YEAR OLDS *cont.*

Friday

Breakfast
Bowl of fresh fruit, e.g. oranges, pineapple and mango
1 pot of fruit yoghurt

Lunchbox
Cheese dip or hummus (see recipe page 122), breadsticks
Raw vegetable sticks, e.g. carrot, pepper and cucumber
Small box of raisins
Milkshake

Supper
Chicken in tomato sauce (see recipe page 87)
Boiled rice, peas
Fresh fruit

Saturday

Breakfast
Boiled egg and wholemeal toast
Orange juice

Lunch
Potato soup (see recipe page 110)
Grated cheese
Granary roll
Fresh fruit salad

Supper
Homemade chicken nuggets (see recipe page 86)
Mighty root mash (see recipe page 107)
Carrots and peas
Baked rice pudding (see recipe page 119)

Sunday

Breakfast
Pancakes filled with apple purée (see recipe page 117)

Lunch
Jacket potato
Grilled chicken
Broccoli and carrots
Raspberry fool (see recipe page 11)

Supper
1 slice of homemade pizza (see recipe pages 96-7)
Salad, e.g. cherry tomatoes, peppers, grated carrot, cucumber
A little salad dressing
Fresh fruit

SEVEN-DAY MENU PLAN FOR 10–15-YEAR OLDS

Monday

Breakfast
Porridge made with milk and water
Raisins

Lunchbox
Bagel with low-fat soft cheese and tinned salmon or tuna
Cherry tomatoes
1 pot of yoghurt
Fresh fruit
Bottle of water

Dinner
Vegetable soup with pasta (see recipe page 112)
Wholemeal roll
Raspberry fool (see recipe page 11)

Tuesday

Breakfast
English muffin or bagel with jam or honey
Yoghurt or milk

Lunchbox
Small container of pasta salad with tuna
Satsuma or kiwi fruit
Small bag or pot of nuts and raisins
Fruit juice

Dinner
Fabulous fish pie (see recipe page 89)
Broccoli and carrots
Baked bananas (see recipe page 120)

Wednesday

Breakfast
Wholegrain cereal with milk
Fresh fruit
Wholemeal toast and honey

Lunchbox
Wholemeal roll with turkey and cranberry sauce
Crudités, e.g. cucumber, pepper and carrot strips
Cheese portion
Piece of fresh fruit
Bottle of water

Dinner
Pasta with sweetcorn and tuna (see recipe page 91)
Brussels sprouts or broccoli
Pancakes (see recipe page 117)

Thursday

Breakfast
Mango and strawberry smoothie (see recipe page 130)

Lunchbox
Thermos of tomato or vegetable soup
Wholemeal roll with cheese
Small bag of dried apricots
Bottle of water

Dinner
Grilled chicken
Jacket potato
Baby sweetcorn and sugar snap peas

SEVEN-DAY MENU PLAN FOR 10–15-YEAR OLDS *cont*

Friday

Breakfast	Muesli with milk or yoghurt Strawberries or raspberries
Lunchbox	Wholemeal egg and mayonnaise sandwich Cucumber slices Carton of yoghurt Banana muffin (see recipe page 124) Bottle of water
Dinner	Mini fish cakes (see recipe page 95) Carrots and peas Banana bread pudding (see recipe page 119)

Saturday

Breakfast	Pancakes filled with fresh fruit (see recipe page 117)
Lunch	Butternut squash soup (see recipe page 111) Wholemeal roll Fresh fruit salad with frozen yoghurt
Dinner	Pasta turkey bolognese (see recipe page 88) Broccoli and cauliflower Best apple crumble (see recipe page 118)

Sunday

Breakfast	Boiled egg and wholemeal toast Nectarine or a pear
Lunch	Golden chicken (see recipe page 89) Mashed potatoes and green beans Fresh fruit salad with frozen yoghurt or custard
Dinner	Sardines on wholemeal toast Baked beans and coleslaw Yoghurt and fruit pudding (see recipe page 120)

SEVEN-DAY VEGETARIAN MENU PLAN FOR 5–10-YEAR OLDS *cont*

Monday

Breakfast
Muesli with milk or yoghurt
Orange juice

Lunchbox
Spicy bean burger (see recipe page 99) wrapped in foil
Small wholemeal roll
Crudités, e.g. carrots, peppers, cucumber
A piece of fruit
Carton of yoghurt
Bottle of water

Dinner
Veggie spaghetti bolognese (see recipe page 98)
Fresh fruit with custard or frozen yoghurt

Tuesday

Breakfast
Porridge made with milk, water, honey
Raisins

Lunchbox
Wholemeal peanut butter and cucumber sandwich
Small bag of dried apricots
Novelty cheese portion
Orange juice

Dinner
Broccoli and cheese soup (see recipe page 111)
Wholemeal roll
Baked bananas with chocolate buttons (see recipe page 24)

Wednesday

Breakfast
Banana milkshake (see recipe page 129)
Wholemeal toast and Marmite

Lunchbox
Mini-bagel filled with soft cheese and banana
Satsuma
Carton of custard
Orange juice

Dinner
Potato and cheese pie (see recipe page 109)
Green beans and carrots
Baked rice pudding with fresh fruit (see recipe page 119)

Thursday

Breakfast
Wholegrain cereal with milk
Orange juice

Lunchbox
Hummus dip (see recipe page 122)
Breadsticks or crackers
Crudités, e.g. carrot, pepper and cucumber strips
Small pot of fruit purée
Carton of fromage frais
Bottle of water

Dinner
Spicy lentil burgers (see recipe page 100)
Jacket potato
Baked beans and broccoli
Fresh fruit salad

SEVEN-DAY VEGETARIAN MENU PLAN FOR 5–10-YEAR OLDS *cont*

Friday

Breakfast
Wholemeal toast and jam or marmalade
Fresh fruit, e.g. apple or strawberries
Milk or yoghurt

Lunchbox
Mini-pitta with grated cheese and tomato
Small pot of nuts, e.g. almonds, cashews, peanuts
Piece of fresh fruit
Apple muffin (see recipe page 123)
Bottle of water

Dinner
Marvellous macaroni cheese with peas (see recipe page 101)
Cauliflower and broccoli
Raspberry fool (see recipe page 11)

Saturday

Breakfast
Poached egg
Tomatoes
Wholemeal toast with Marmite

Lunch
Carrot soup (see recipe page 112) with grated cheese
Wholemeal roll
Baked apple stuffed with raisins, chopped dates, almonds and honey

Dinner
Butter bean and leeks (see recipe page 105)
New potatoes and carrots
Yoghurt

Sunday

Breakfast
Pancakes filled with fresh fruit (see recipe page 117)
Orange juice

Lunch
Nut burgers (see recipe page 100)
Jacket potato
Carrots and brussels sprouts or broccoli
Banana bread pudding (see recipe page 119)

Dinner
Cheese on wholemeal toast
Tomatoes and cucumber
Yoghurt

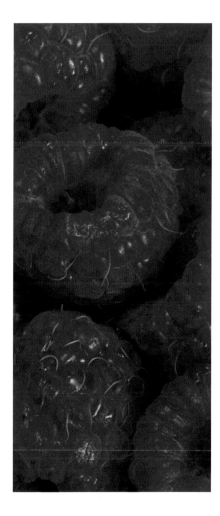

SEVEN-DAY VEGETARIAN MENU PLAN FOR 10–15 YEAR OLDS *cont*

Monday

Breakfast
English muffin or bagel with a slice of cheese
Fresh fruit

Lunchbox
Pot of pasta salad with red kidney beans, peppers and tomatoes
Carton of yoghurt
Small bag of dried fruit
Bottle of water

Dinner
Cauliflower cheese
Jacket potato and green beans
Baked bananas with chocolate buttons (see recipe page 24)

Tuesday

Breakfast
Wholegrain cereal with milk
Raisins or dried apricots

Lunchbox
Wholemeal roll with sliced avocado and tomato
Cheese portion
Piece of fresh fruit
Carton of milkshake

Dinner
Cheese and tomato pizza (see recipe page 97) with any of the suggested toppings
Jacket potato
Coleslaw
Fresh fruit

Wednesday

Breakfast
Porridge made with milk and water
Banana

Lunchbox
Thermos of vegetable soup
Wholemeal roll
Small bunch of seedless grapes
Orange juice

Dinner
Pasta with chickpeas and spinach (see recipe page 102)
Fresh fruit salad with yoghurt or custard

Thursday

Breakfast
Muesli mixed with grated apple
Milk or yoghurt

Lunchbox
Cooked vegetarian sausage, wrapped in foil
Wholemeal Marmite sandwich
Small pot of nuts, e.g. almonds, cashews, peanuts
Carton of fromage frais
Bottle of water

Dinner
Burritos filled with beans (see recipe page 104)
Salad or broccoli
Stewed pears with raisins and honey

SEVEN-DAY VEGETARIAN MENU PLAN FOR 10–15 YEAR OLDS *cont*

Friday

Breakfast	Fruit smoothie (see recipe page 73) Wholemeal toast
Lunchbox	English muffin with peanut butter and cheese Carrot sticks Carton of yoghurt Small bag of dried fruit Fruit juice
Dinner	Vegetable korma (see recipe page 106) Rice Fresh fruit salad

Saturday

Breakfast	Scrambled egg with mushrooms Wholemeal toast
Lunch	Spicy bean burger (see recipe page 99) Wholemeal bap Salad Fresh fruit
Dinner	Jacket potato filled with stir-fried vegetables or ratatouille Best apple crumble (or other fruit variety) (see recipe page 118) Custard or yoghurt

Sunday

Breakfast	Pancakes filled with sliced bananas and honey (see recipe page 117)
Lunch	Mild spiced red lentils (see recipe page 105) Rice Carrots and broccoli Baked custard with cherries (see recipe page 121)
Dinner	Real tomato soup (see recipe page 110) with grated cheese Wholemeal roll Fresh fruit

home-made chicken nuggets

These home-made chicken nuggets are far healthier than the shop-bought and takeaway versions. The wheatgerm used for the coating provides essential B vitamins (thiamin and niacin), iron and zinc. They're baked rather than fried, which reduces the fat content and makes them tasty without artificial flavour-enhancers.

MAKES 4 SERVINGS

- 3 chicken breasts, boneless, skinned
- 85 g (3 oz) wheatgerm or breadcrumbs
- ½ tsp (2.5 ml) salt
- ¼ tsp (1.25 ml) garlic powder
- Freshly ground black pepper
- 90 ml (3 fl oz) water
- 1 egg white

Great source of **protein, B vitamins** *and* **fibre**

1 Pre-heat the oven to 200 °C/400 °F/Gas mark 6.
2 Cut the chicken breasts into small chunks.
3 Combine the wheatgerm, salt, garlic powder and a little pepper. Place the mixture in a large plastic bag.
4 Combine the water and egg white in a bowl. Dip the chicken pieces into the egg mixture, and then drop into the plastic bag. Shake until the chicken is thoroughly coated.
5 Place the coated chicken pieces on an oiled baking tray. Bake for 10–15 minutes or until tender and golden brown, turning once midway through cooking.

chicken burgers

These are a nutritious alternative to the beef variety due to their lower fat content. Unlike traditional burgers, they're dry-fried so they don't absorb lots of oil.

MAKES 4 BURGERS

- 1 onion, finely chopped
- 1 stick celery, finely chopped
- 1 clove garlic, crushed
- 2 tbsp (30 ml) olive oil
- 2 chicken breasts, skinless and boneless
- 2 tbsp (30 ml) fresh parsley, chopped (or 1 tbsp/15 ml dried parsley)
- 60 g (2 oz) fresh breadcrumbs
- Salt and freshly ground black pepper
- 1 egg yolk
- Flour for coating

Great source of **B vitamins**, **fibre** *and heart-healthy* **monounsaturated** *fats*

1 Sauté the onion, celery and garlic in the olive oil for 5 minutes. Meanwhile mince or finely chop the chicken in a food processor.
2 Combine the onion mixture, chicken, parsley and breadcrumbs in a bowl. Season with salt and pepper and bind the mixture together with the egg yolk.
3 Form into four burgers, roll in the flour and dry-fry in a non-stick pan over a medium heat until golden and cooked thoroughly, turning halfway through (about 5–6 minutes each side).

chicken in tomato sauce

Anything in tomato sauce will be a hit with most children so this chicken dish could help you disguise extra vegetables.

Super-rich in **antioxidants**

MAKES 4 SERVINGS

- 4 chicken portions, on the bone
- 2 tbsp (30 ml) olive oil
- 1 onion, chopped
- 2 garlic cloves, crushed
- 1 red and 1 green pepper, chopped
- 1 tin (400 g) chopped tomatoes
- 1 tbsp (15 ml) each of fresh basil, fresh parsley and fresh chives (alternatively, use 1 tbsp/15 ml dried mixed herbs)

1 *Pre-heat the oven to 160 °C/325 °F/Gas mark 3.*
2 *Sauté the chicken portions in 1 tablespoon of the olive oil until browned. Remove with a slotted spoon and put in a casserole dish.*
3 *Heat the remaining oil. Add the onion and garlic and cook for 3 minutes.*
4 *Add the peppers and cook for a further 2 minutes. Add the tinned tomatoes and herbs and simmer for 5 minutes.*
5 *Spoon sauce over the chicken and cook in the oven for about 45 minutes.*

chicken curry with veggies

Make this dish more nutritious by adding extra vegetables to the curry sauce. You can adjust the amount of curry paste according to your children's tastes.

MAKES 4 SERVINGS

- 1 tbsp (15 ml) olive oil
- 2 chicken breasts, boneless, skinned and cut into strips
- 1 onion, chopped
- 1 clove of garlic, crushed
- 2 tbsp (30 ml) mild curry paste
- 1 tin (400 g) chopped tomatoes
- 125 g (4 oz) cauliflower florets
- 125 g (4 oz) carrots, sliced
- 125 g (4 oz) frozen peas
- 60g (2oz) sultanas

Rich in **protein**, **B vitamins** *and* **antioxidants**

1 *Heat the olive oil in a large heavy bottomed pan and cook the chicken strips for 5 minutes until brown. Put aside on a plate.*
2 *Add the onion and sauté for 5 minutes.*
3 *Add the curry paste, tinned tomatoes and vegetables, stir then bring to the boil. Simmer for 10 minutes.*
4 *Return the chicken to the pan with the sultanas, and continue cooking for a further 10 minutes.*

lean meat burgers

These home-made meat burgers are made with lean mince and cooked without extra oil. This means they're low in fat – plus as they're home-made you know exactly what's in them!

MAKES 8 SMALL OR 4 LARGE BURGERS

Low in fat and a **good source** *of* **iron**

- 350 g (12 oz) extra lean minced meat (beef, turkey, pork)
- 60 g (2 oz) dried breadcrumbs
- 3 tbsp (45 ml) water
- 1 small onion, chopped
- 2 tbsp (30 ml) fresh sage or parsley, chopped (or 1 tbsp/15 ml dried herbs)
- Freshly ground black pepper

1 *Place the minced meat, breadcrumbs, water, onion, herbs and pepper in a bowl. Mix well to combine.*

2 *Divide the mixture into 4 or 8 balls and flatten into burgers. Dry fry in a hot non-stick pan for 3–4 minutes each side. Alternatively, place the burgers on a baking sheet and cook in the oven at 200°C/400°F/Gas mark 6 for 10–15 minutes depending on the size of the burgers.*

3 *Test by inserting a skewer into the middle of a burger – there should be no trace of pink in the meat and the juices should run clear.*

pasta turkey bolognese

Turkey mince is used in place of the conventional beef. It's high in protein and low in fat. Bolognese sauce is a tasty way to disguise vegetables and beans.

MAKES 4 SERVINGS

Good source of **zinc**, **iron** *and* **beta carotene**

- 1 tbsp (15 ml) olive oil
- 300 g (10 oz) turkey mince
- 1 large onion, chopped
- 2 sticks of celery
- 2 carrots, grated
- 1 tin (400 g) chopped tomatoes
- 1 tin (420 g) red kidney beans
- 1 teaspoon (5 ml) dried mixed herbs
- Salt and freshly ground black pepper
- 175 g (6 oz) spaghetti or other pasta shapes (adjust the quantity according to your children's appetite)

1 *Heat the olive oil in a large pan and sauté the turkey mince until it is browned. Add the onions and cook for a further 3–4 minutes.*

2 *Add the celery and carrots and cook for a further 5 minutes until just tender.*

3 *Stir in the chopped tomatoes, red kidney beans and herbs. Bring to the boil and simmer for 5 minutes. Season with salt and black pepper.*

4 *Meanwhile, cook the pasta according to the directions on the packet. Drain, then stir into the Bolognese sauce.*

golden chicken

This is one of the easiest and healthiest ways to cook chicken and proves that you don't need fast food to tempt kids to the table.

MAKES 4 SERVINGS

- 4 chicken breasts, boneless and skinless
- 60 g (2 oz) flour
- 1 tbsp (15 ml) paprika
- 2 tbsp (30 ml) olive oil
- Salt and freshly ground black pepper to taste

*Good source of **protein** and **monounsaturated** fats*

1 *Pre-heat the oven to 180 °C/350 °F/Gas mark 4.*

2 *Place flour and paprika in a plastic bag. Add the chicken breasts and shake until the chicken is well coated.*

3 *Put the olive oil in a baking dish. Add the chicken breasts and turn carefully in the oil. Cover with foil and bake for 20 minutes.*

4 *Remove the foil and bake for a further 10 minutes until the chicken is golden brown.*

fabulous fish pie

This popular children's meal is made healthier by adding swede to the mashed potato. Alternatively, substitute parsnips or squash if you prefer.

MAKES 4 SERVINGS

- 300 g (10 oz) potatoes, peeled and cut into large chunks
- 300 g (10 oz) swede, peeled and cut into large chunks
- 550 g (1¼ lb) cod fillets
- 600ml (1 pint) skimmed milk
- 1 bay leaf
- 25 g (1 oz) butter
- 2 large leeks, thinly sliced
- 2 heaped tbsp plain flour
- Salt, freshly ground black pepper, 1 tsp (5 ml) Dijon mustard
- 60 g (2 oz) mature Cheddar cheese, grated

*Rich in **fibre**, **calcium** and **vitamin C***

1 *Pre-heat the oven to 190 °C/375 °F/Gas mark 5.*

2 *Cook the potatoes and swede in boiling water for about 15 minutes or until soft. Drain and mash with about one third of the milk.*

3 *Meanwhile place the cod in a saucepan with the remaining milk and bay leaf. Bring to the boil and simmer for about 5 minutes.*

4 *Strain the milk into a jug. Roughly flake the fish.*

5 *Melt the butter in a pan, add the leeks and cook for 5 minutes until softened. Stir in the flour. Slowly add the milk, stirring continuously over a low heat until the sauce has thickened. Season with salt, pepper and Dijon mustard.*

6 *Combine the sauce with the leeks and fish. Place in a baking dish.*

7 *Cover evenly with the mashed potatoes and swede and scatter the cheese on top.*

8 *Bake for 20 minutes until the top is golden brown.*

mini chicken and vegetable parcels

These little pies are made with filo pastry, which contains less fat than shortcrust pastry. You can substitute different vegetables for those suggested in the recipe – they'll count towards the 5 daily servings of vegetables and fruit recommended for children.

MAKES 8 SMALL PARCELS

- 2 chicken breasts, skinless and boneless
- 2 tbsp (30 ml) olive oil
- 85 g (3 oz) button mushrooms, sliced
- 1 medium courgette, chopped
- 2 carrots, thinly sliced
- 2 tsp (10 ml) cornflour
- 200 ml (7 fl oz) milk
- 175 g (6 oz) filo pastry

Good source of **protein** *and* **complex carbohydrates** *plus* **beta-carotene**

1 *Cut the chicken into small pieces. Heat 1 tbsp of the oil in a pan. Add the chicken and sauté over a high heat for 3 minutes.*
2 *Add the vegetables and continue cooking over a moderate heat for 5–6 minutes until the vegetables are softened.*
3 *Stir in the cornflour. Slowly add the milk, stirring continuously until the sauce has thickened. Remove from the heat.*
4 *Cut the pastry into 24 squares each measuring 13 cm × 13 cm (5 in × 5 in). Lightly brush one square with olive oil, cover with another square and brush with oil. Cover with a third square.*

5 *Place a spoonful of the filling in the centre of the square. Brush the edges with a little water. Fold over one corner of the pastry to make a triangle and press to seal. Repeat with the remaining pastry squares until you have 8 parcels.*
6 *Place the parcels on a lightly oiled baking tray and brush with olive oil. Bake in the oven for 15–20 minutes until golden brown.*

toad-and-veggies-in-the-hole

This variation of Toad-in-the-Hole includes tasty root vegetables, which add extra vitamins and fibre to the meal. It is a good dish to serve to vegetarians, too, as you can substitute vegetarian sausages for the meat ones.

Rich in **iron**, **beta carotene** *and* **calcium**

MAKES 4 SERVINGS

- 4 carrots
- 1 parsnip
- 225 g (8 oz) butternut squash
- 2 tbsp (30 ml) sunflower oil
- 4 lean beef sausages or vegetarian sausages
- 125 g (4 oz) plain flour
- 1 egg
- 300 ml (½ pint) milk

1 *Pre-heat the oven to 190 °C/375 °F/ Gas mark 5.*

2 *Cut the vegetables into 2½ cm (1 in) chunks. Place in a roasting tin, drizzle over the sunflower oil and toss to coat. Bake in the oven for 20 minutes.*

3 *Prick the sausages. Add to the roasting tin and cook in the oven for a further 10 minutes.*

4 *Meanwhile make the batter. Place the flour, egg and milk in a liquidiser and blend until smooth.*

5 *Spoon the roasted vegetables and sausages into a rectangular dish. Pour over the batter and bake for a further 40 minutes until the batter has risen and is crisp on the outside.*

pasta with sweetcorn and tuna

This dish is quick to prepare and makes a good midweek standby. It's also good eaten cold as a lunchbox salad.

MAKES 4 SERVINGS

- 175 g (6 oz) pasta shapes (adjust the quantity according to your children's appetite)
- 1 tbsp (15 ml) olive oil
- 1 onion, chopped
- 1 garlic clove, crushed
- 1 tin (400 g) chopped tomatoes
- 1 tbsp (15 ml) tomato purée
- 125 g (4 oz) sweetcorn
- 1 tin (200 g) tuna in water or brine, drained and flaked
- 1 tsp (5 ml) dried basil

Provides **protein**, **complex carbohydrates** *and* **fibre**

1 *Cook the pasta according to the directions on the packet. Drain.*

2 *Meanwhile, place the onion, garlic and tomatoes in a large non-stick frying pan and cook for 4–5 minutes until onion is soft.*

3 *Stir in the tomato purée, chopped tomatoes and sweetcorn and cook for 5 minutes.*

4 *Add the tuna and basil and heat through.*

5 *Stir the sweetcorn and tuna sauce into the pasta and serve.*

pasta with ham and mushroom sauce

MAKES 4 SERVINGS

- 175 g (6 oz) pasta shells (adjust quantity depending on appetite)
- 1 tbsp (15 ml) olive oil
- 4 slices (125 g) ham (preferably reduced salt), chopped
- 125 g (4 oz) small mushrooms, halved
- 1 tbsp (15 ml) cornflour
- 300ml (½ pint) milk
- 1 tsp (5ml) dried oregano
- Freshly ground black pepper

Good source of **complex carbohydrates**, **protein** *and* **calcium**

1 Cook the pasta according to directions on the packet. Drain.
2 Meanwhile, heat the olive oil in a large frying pan. Cook the ham and mushrooms for 4–5 minutes.
3 Stir in the cornflour together with a little milk. Gradually add the rest of the milk, stirring continuously.
4 Heat until the sauce just reaches boiling point. Remove from the heat and stir in the herbs and pepper.
5 Combine with the cooked pasta.

pasta and tuna bake

This recipe makes a balanced meal in itself. The tuna and milk provide protein, the pasta provides energy-giving carbohydrate and the vegetables provide vitamins and fibre.

MAKES 4 SERVINGS

- 175 g (6 oz) pasta shells (adjust the quantity according to appetite)
- 1 tbsp (15 ml) olive oil
- 1 onion, sliced
- 2 sticks of celery, chopped
- 1 green pepper, chopped
- 125 g (4 oz) frozen peas
- 1 tbsp (15 ml) fresh parsley, chopped
- 1 tin (200g) tuna in water or brine

Full of **protein**, **fibre**, **vitamins** *and* **calcium**

White Sauce:
- 1 tbsp (15 ml) butter
- 1 tbsp (15 ml) cornflour
- 300 ml (½ pint) milk

1 Pre-heat the oven to 190 °C/375 °F/Gas mark 5.
2 Cook the pasta. Drain.
3 In a non-stick frying pan, heat the olive oil. Sauté the onion for 3 mins until translucent, then celery, pepper and peas. Continue cooking for a further 5 mins.
4 White sauce: melt butter in a pan, stir in cornflour, then add the milk slowly, stirring over a low/medium heat until thickened.
5 Spread a thin layer of vegetables onto the bottom of a baking dish. Cover with a layer of pasta, then flaked tuna. Add a layer of white sauce. Sprinkle parsley between each layer. Repeat the process. Finish with white sauce on top.
6 Bake for 20 minutes.

lasagne

Choosing lean mince keeps the saturated fat content of this recipe to a minimum. Include other varieties of vegetables, such as mushrooms and spinach, instead of the celery and pepper, if you wish. This dish is a good way of hiding those vegetables!

MAKES 4 SERVINGS

Rich in **vitamins**, **fibre** *and* **calcium**

- 1 tbsp (15 ml) olive oil
- 1 onion, chopped
- 1 celery stick, chopped
- 1 red pepper, chopped
- 225 g (8 oz) lean beef mince (or turkey mince)
- 1 tin (400g) chopped tomatoes
- 2 tbsp (30 ml) tomato puree
- 1 tsp (5 ml) dried basil or oregano
- Salt and freshly ground black pepper to taste
- 8 sheets lasagne (the no pre-cook variety)
- 85 g (3 oz) mozzarella cheese

1 *Pre-heat the oven to 180 °C/350 °F/Gas mark 4.*

2 *Heat the olive oil in a large non-stick frying pan. Cook the onion, celery, pepper and mince, stirring frequently, for 5–6 minutes until the mince is browned. Drain off any fat.*

3 *Add the tomatoes, tomato puree, and herbs. Season with salt and pepper to taste.*

4 *Place a layer of lasagne sheets at the bottom of an oiled baking dish. Spoon over one third of the mince mixture. Repeat the layers, finishing with a layer of the mince mixture.*

5 *Cover with very thin slices of mozzarella. Bake for 30 minutes until the cheese is bubbling and golden.*

easy chilli

This version of the classic dish smuggles in extra vegetables. You may use any type of lean minced meat such as turkey, beef or pork.

MAKES 4 SERVINGS

- 225 g (8 oz) lean minced turkey, beef or pork
- 1 tbsp (15 ml) olive oil
- 1 onion, chopped
- 1 garlic clove, crushed
- 1 green pepper, chopped
- 1 celery stick, chopped
- 85 g (3 oz) button mushrooms, whole or cut in half
- 1 tsp (5 ml) paprika
- 1 pinch chilli powder (according to your children's tastes)
- ½ tsp (2.5 ml) ground cumin
- 2 tbsp (30 ml) tomato puree

Rich in **iron**, **zinc** *and* **fibre**

- 400 ml (¾ pint) stock or water
- 1 tin (420g) red kidney beans

1 *Dry-fry the mince in a non-stick pan for about 5 minutes until browned. Drain off any fat. Set aside.*

2 *Heat the olive oil in a large pan and sauté the onion, pepper, celery, mushrooms and garlic for about 3 minutes. Add the spices and fry for a further minute.*

3 *Add the tomato puree, stock or water, and the beans. Cover and simmer for about 1 hour.*

risotto with chicken and veggies

Peppers are bursting with vitamin C and other antioxidants. This recipe is a delicious way of introducing them to children.

MAKES 4 SERVINGS

Packed with **protein** *and* **antioxidants**

- 1 tbsp (15 ml) olive oil
- 1 onion, chopped
- 1 red pepper, cut into thin strips
- 1 yellow pepper, cut into thin strips
- 175 g (6 oz) long-grain or Arborio rice
- 1 l (1.6 pints) chicken or vegetable stock
- 125 g (4 oz) cooked chicken, chopped
- 25 g (1 oz) Parmesan cheese, grated
- Handful of fresh chives or parsley, if available

1 Heat the olive oil in a large saucepan.
2 Sauté the onion and peppers over a moderate heat for about 7 minutes.
3 Add the rice and cook for 2–3 minutes until the rice is translucent. Add the stock and bring to the boil, partially cover with a lid, and simmer for 12–15 minutes until the rice is tender and the liquid has been absorbed. Add a little more stock if the risotto becomes dry.
4 Add the chicken and half the Parmesan. Heat through for a few minutes.
5 Serve topped with the remaining Parmesan and herbs.

risotto with haddock

MAKES 4 SERVINGS

A vitamin-rich dish

- 2 tbsp (30 ml) olive oil
- 1 onion, chopped
- 175 g (6 oz) long-grain or Arborio rice
- 600 ml (1 pint) vegetable stock*
- 1 bay leaf
- 350 g (12 oz) frozen or smoked haddock fillet, thawed
- 200 g (7 oz) frozen peas
- Salt and freshly ground black pepper

*Alternatively, use 2 tsp (10ml) Swiss vegetable bouillon powder, or 1 vegetable stock cube dissolved in 600 ml (1 pint) water

1 Heat the olive oil in a large saucepan. Add the rice and onion and sauté for 2–3 minutes until the rice is translucent.
2 Place the rice in a large pan with the stock and add the bay leaf. Bring to the boil. Cover and simmer for 15 minutes.
3 Add the haddock and peas and continue cooking for a further 5 minutes until the liquid has been absorbed and the fish flakes easily. Roughly break up the fish and stir the rice mixture to distribute evenly.

mini fish cakes

All fish is rich in protein and important minerals. Salmon, in particular, is rich in the essential omega-3 fatty acids, important for brain development and physical activity.

MAKES 4 LARGE OR 8 SMALL FISH CAKES

- 450 g (1 lb) potatoes, peeled
- 450 g (1 lb) salmon or cod fillet, skinned
- 60 g (2 oz) butter
- 4 tbsp (60 ml) milk
- 1 tbsp (15 ml) fresh parsley, chopped
- Salt and freshly ground black pepper

1 *Cut the potatoes into quarters and boil for 15 minutes until soft. Drain.*
2 *Meanwhile, poach the fish in water for 10 minutes. Drain and flake the fish, carefully removing all the bones.*

Rich in **omega-3 fatty acids** *and* **minerals**

3 *Mash the potatoes with the butter, milk, parsley and salt and pepper. Mix in the flaked fish. Shape into 4 or 8 cakes.*
4 *Shallow fry in olive oil for a few minutes on each side. Drain on kitchen paper.*

bean and tuna salad

MAKES 4 SERVINGS

- 1 tin (420g) cannelini or butter beans, drained
- 2 tomatoes, cubed
- 1 tin (100 g) tuna in brine, drained and flaked
- 125 g (4 oz) green beans, cooked and cooled
- 1 tbsp (15 ml) red wine vinegar
- 2 tbsp (30 ml) olive oil
- Handful of fresh herbs: chives, parsley

Full of **protein**, **B vitamins**, **iron** *and* **fibre**

1 *Combine the tinned beans, tomatoes, tuna and green beans in a bowl.*
2 *Mix together the vinegar, oil and herbs and combine with the salad.*

pizzas

Making your own pizzas is easy if you have a bread machine. Alternatively, use the quick pizza base recipe, as this doesn't require kneading or proving. If you haven't got time to make your own tomato sauce, use a jar of pasta sauce but remember it contains quite a lot of salt. Children will enjoy adding their own toppings, too.

MAKES 1 LARGE PIZZA OR 8 SMALL PIZZAS

Pizza base:
- 225 g (8 oz) strong white flour
- ½ sachet easy-blend yeast
- ½ tsp (2.5ml) salt
- 175 ml (6 fl oz) warm water
- 1 tbsp (15 ml) olive oil

Great source **protein, calcium** *and* **antioxidants**

1 *If making the dough by hand, mix the flour, yeast and salt in a large bowl. Make a well in the centre and add the oil and half the water. Stir with a wooden spoon, gradually adding more liquid until you have a pliable dough. Turn the dough out onto a floured surface and knead for about 5 minutes until you have a smooth and elastic dough. Place the dough in a clean, lightly oiled bowl, cover with a tea towel and leave in a warm place for about 1 hour or until doubled in size.*
2 *If you are using a bread machine, place the ingredients in the tin and follow the instructions supplied with the machine.*
3 *Turn out the dough; knead briefly before rolling out on a surface to the desired shape. Alternatively, divide the dough into 8 pieces then roll each one into a circle approximately 10 cm (4 inches) diameter.*
4 *Transfer to an oiled pizza pan or baking tray and finish shaping by hand. The dough should be approx.*

5 mm (¼ in) thick. For a thicker crust, let the dough rise for 30 minutes, otherwise the pizza is now ready for topping and baking.
5 *Bake on the top shelf of the oven at 220 °C/425 °F/ Gas mark 7 for 15–20 minutes or until the topping is bubbling and the crust is golden brown.*

Quick Pizza Base
- 225 g (8 oz) self-raising white flour
- 1 tsp (5 ml) baking powder
- ½ tsp (2.5 ml) salt
- 40 g (1½ oz) butter or margarine
- 150 ml (5 fl oz) skimmed milk

1 *Mix the flour, baking powder and salt in a bowl.*
2 *Rub in the butter or margarine until the mixture resembles breadcrumbs.*
3 *Add the milk, quickly mixing with a fork, just until the mixture comes together.*
4 *Roll or press the dough into a circle approx 25 cm (10 in) in diameter or shape into 8 circles approx 7 cm (3 in) diameter and transfer onto a baking tray or pizza pan.*
5 *The base is now ready for topping. Bake on the top shelf of the oven at 220 °C/425 °F/Gas mark 7 for 15 minutes for a large pizza or 10 minutes for smaller pizzas.*

cheese and tomato pizza

Tomato sauce
- 1 tbsp (15 ml) olive oil
- 1 small onion, finely chopped
- 1 garlic clove, crushed
- 300 ml (½ pint) passata (smooth sieved tomatoes) or 1 tin (400 g) chopped tomatoes
- 1 tbsp (15 ml) tomato puree
- 1 tsp (5 ml) dried basil
- ½ tsp (2.5 ml) sugar
- Pinch of salt and freshly ground black pepper
- 125 g (4 oz) mozzarella, sliced (or grated Cheddar cheese)

Rich in **antioxidants** *and* **calcium**

1 *Sauté the onion and garlic in the olive oil for 5 minutes until translucent.*
2 *Add the passata or chopped tomatoes, tomato purée, basil, sugar, salt and pepper. Continue to simmer for 5–10 minutes or until the sauce has thickened a little.*
3 *Spread the sauce on the pizza base. Scatter over the cheese and any additional toppings from the list below.*
4 *Bake at 230 °C/450 °F/Gas mark 8 for 15–20 minutes until the cheese is bubbling and golden brown.*

Pizza toppings
This is a great opportunity to add extra vegetables to your children's diet. Add any combination of the following:
- tomatoes, sliced
- cherry tomatoes, halved
- red, yellow and green peppers, sliced
- mushrooms, sliced
- sweetcorn
- onion rings
- olives
- courgettes, sliced
- tuna, flaked
- spinach, cooked and drained
- broccoli florets, cooked
- colourful cheeses, e.g. Red Leicester, Double Gloucester
- pineapple
- peas
- leeks, thinly sliced
- baby sweetcorn
- cooked turkey or chicken
- spring onions
- cooked aubergine
- poached egg on top
- salmon (smoked or tinned) and dill
- basil
- oregano

Alternative Pizza Bases
- Ready-made pizza base
- English muffin, toasted and split horizontally
- Foccacia bread, halved horizontally
- Ciabatta loaf, halved horizontally
- Wholemeal or white pitta bread, split horizontally
- French bread, sliced in half horizontally

veggie spaghetti bolognese

Lentils are substituted for the meat in the Bolognese sauce. They provide plenty of protein, iron, fibre and B vitamins and make a super-tasty main course.

MAKES 4 SERVINGS

Good source of **fibre**, **vitamins** *and* **minerals**

- 1 tbsp (15 ml) olive oil
- 1 onion, chopped
- 2 carrots, grated
- 1 large courgette, finely chopped
- 1 tin (400g) chopped tomatoes
- 1 tin (420g) green lentils (or 125 g (4 oz) dried lentils, soaked and cooked)
- 1 tsp (5 ml) dried mixed herbs
- 175 g (6 oz) spaghetti (adjust quantity depending on appetite)
- 1 tbsp (15 ml) olive oil
- 2 tbsp (30 ml) Parmesan cheese, grated

1 Heat the olive oil in a large frying pan. Add the vegetables, stirring often for about 5 minutes, until softened.

2 Add the tomatoes, lentils and herbs. Cook for a further 5–10 minutes until the sauce thickens slightly.

3 Meanwhile, cook the spaghetti in boiling water according to the directions on the packet. Drain and toss in a little olive oil.

4 Divide the spaghetti between 4 bowls. Spoon over the Bolognese sauce and sprinkle on the Parmesan cheese.

pasta with tomato and peppers

This is one of the quickest stand-by dishes in my house! You can add other vegetables, such as mushrooms, courgettes or green beans to the tomato sauce instead of peppers.

MAKES 4 SERVINGS

- 1 tbsp (15 ml) olive oil
- 1 onion, chopped
- 2 garlic cloves, crushed
- 1 red or green pepper, chopped
- 1 tin (400g) chopped tomatoes
- 2 tbsp (30 ml) tomato puree
- 1 tsp (5 ml) dried basil
- Salt and freshly ground black pepper
- Pinch of sugar
- 175 g (6 oz) pasta shells (adjust quantity depending on appetite)
- 85 g (3 oz) Cheddar cheese, grated

1 Heat the olive oil in a large frying pan. Add the onions, garlic and peppers and sauté for 5 minutes or until the vegetables have softened.

2 Add the tomatoes, tomato puree, basil, salt, pepper and sugar. Cook for 5 minutes or until the sauce thickens slightly.

Full of **antioxidants**

3 Meanwhile, cook the pasta shells in boiling water according to the directions on the packet. Drain.

4 Combine the sauce with the pasta. Spoon into 4 dishes and sprinkle over the cheese.

spicy bean burgers

This is a favourite teatime recipe that even my children's non-vegetarian friends enjoy. The beans are a good source of protein, iron and B vitamins, but you can use other beans, such as butter beans, flageolet or cannelloni beans instead. You can hide lots of vegetables in the burgers, too.

MAKES 8 SMALL OR 4 LARGE BURGERS

- 2 tins (400 g × 2) red kidney beans
- 1 tbsp (15 ml) olive oil
- 1 onion, chopped
- 1 clove of garlic, crushed
- 1 celery stick, chopped
- 1 carrot, finely grated
- 1 green pepper, chopped
- ½ tsp (2.5 ml) ground cumin
- ½ tsp (2.5 ml) ground coriander
- 1 tbsp (15 ml) tomato purée
- 1 tbsp (15ml) fresh coriander, chopped (optional)
- 1 egg
- 60 g (2 oz) dried breadcrumbs
- 60 g (2 oz) Cheddar cheese, grated
- Salt and freshly ground black pepper

Packed with **protein** *and* **fibre**

1 Pre-heat oven to 200 °C/400 °F/Gas mark 6.
2 Drain then mash the beans in a bowl.
3 Heat the oil in a frying pan and sauté the onion for 3–4 minutes until transparent. Add the garlic, celery, carrot, green pepper, spices and cook for a further 5 minutes.
4 Add the mashed beans, tomato purée, egg, breadcrumbs and cheese. Mix together, then shape into 8 small/4 large burgers.
5 Place on an oiled baking tray. Bake in the oven for 25 minutes until golden and crisp.

spicy lentil burgers

These tasty burgers are made with red lentils, a terrific source of protein, iron and fibre. They are oven-baked using only a little oil.

MAKES 8 SMALL OR 4 LARGE BURGERS

- 1 tbsp (15 ml) olive oil
- 1 onion, finely chopped
- 1–2 tsp (5–10 ml) curry powder (depending on your children's tastes)
- 175 g (6 oz) red lentils (dried, no need to soak)
- 600 ml (1 pint) vegetable stock
- 125 g (4 oz) fresh wholemeal breadcrumbs
- Salt and freshly ground black pepper to taste
- A little oil for brushing

Full of **protein** *and* **iron**

1 *Pre-heat the oven to 200 °C/400 °F/Gas mark 6.*
2 *Heat the olive oil in a large pan and sauté the onion until softened. Stir in the curry powder and cook for a further 2 minutes.*
3 *Add the lentils and stock. Bring to the boil and simmer for 20–25 minutes.*
4 *Allow to cool slightly then mix in the breadcrumbs. Shape into 4 or 8 burgers.*
5 *Place on a lightly oiled baking tray and brush each burger with a little oil.*
6 *Bake for 7–10 minutes until golden and firm.*

nut burgers

These delicious burgers are a real hit with my children. Nuts are a terrific source of essential fats, protein, iron, zinc and B vitamins. You can substitute other types of nuts, such as almonds, hazelnuts or peanuts for the cashews if you wish.

MAKES 4 LARGE OR 8 SMALL BURGERS

- 1 onion, chopped
- 1 garlic clove, crushed
- ½ red pepper
- 1 tbsp (15 ml) rapeseed oil
- 1 tsp (5 ml) dried mixed herbs
- 1 tbsp (15 ml) wholemeal flour
- 150 ml (5 fl oz) water
- ½ vegetable stock cube
- 225 g (8 oz) cashew nuts
- 125 g (4 oz) fresh wholemeal breadcrumbs
- Salt and freshly ground black pepper
- A little olive oil for brushing

Full of healthy **monounsaturated fats**, **minerals** *and* **vitamins**

1 *Pre-heat the oven to 200 °C/400 °F/Gas mark 6.*
2 *Sauté the onion, garlic and red pepper in the oil for 5 minutes until translucent. Add the herbs and flour and continue cooking for a further 2 minutes.*
3 *Stir in the water and stock cube and continue stirring until the sauce has thickened.*
4 *Grind the cashews in a food processor then add with the breadcrumbs to the sauce. Season with salt and pepper to taste. Allow to cool slightly.*
5 *Shape into 4–8 burgers and arrange on an oiled baking tray. Brush lightly with a little olive oil. Bake in the oven for 15–20 minutes until golden and crisp on the outside.*

marvellous macaroni cheese with peas

Macaroni cheese is popular with most children. Here's a more nutritious version with peas and mushrooms, but it also works well with broad beans, carrots and red kidney beans.

MAKES 4 SERVINGS

Packed with **calcium** *and* **vitamin C**

- 175 g (6 oz) macaroni (adjust quantity depending on appetite)
- 60 g (2 oz) frozen peas
- 25 g (1 oz) butter
- 60 g (2 oz) button mushrooms, sliced
- 25 g (1 oz) cornflour
- 300 ml (½ pint) milk (full-fat or semi-skimmed)
- ½ tsp (2.5 ml) Dijon mustard
- 85g (3oz) mature Cheddar grated
- Freshly ground black pepper

1 Pre-heat the oven to 200 °C/400 °F/Gas mark 6.
2 Cook the macaroni in boiling water according to the packet, adding the frozen peas during the last 3 minutes of cooking time. Drain.
3 Heat the butter in a pan. Add the mushrooms and sauté for 2 minutes.
4 Blend the cornflour with a little of the milk in a jug. Gradually add the remainder of the milk.
5 Gradually add the milk mixture to the mushrooms in the pan, stirring continuously until the sauce just reaches the boil and has thickened.
6 Remove from the heat, stir in mustard, half the cheese and pepper to taste.
7 Stir in the macaroni and peas. Spoon into an ovenproof dish, sprinkle the remaining cheese over the top and bake for 15–20 minutes until the top is bubbling and golden.

penne with cheese and broccoli

Broccoli is full of vitamin C, folate and other powerful antioxidants. This recipe is a tasty way of getting your children to eat this superfood!

MAKES 4 SERVINGS

- 175 g (6 oz) penne pasta (adjust quantity depending on appetite)
- 225 g (8 oz) broccoli florets
- 1 tbsp (15 ml) olive oil
- 1 large onion, sliced
- 1 tbsp (15 ml) cornflour
- 300 ml (½ pint) milk
- 60 g (2 oz) mature Cheddar cheese

Bursting with **antioxidants**

1 Cook the pasta in boiling water according to the directions on the packet, adding the broccoli during the last 3 minutes of cooking time. Drain.
2 In a non-stick pan, sauté the onion in the olive oil for 5 minutes until softened.
3 Blend the cornflour with a little of the milk in a jug. Gradually add the remainder of the milk. Slowly add to the onion, stirring continuously until the sauce has thickened. Stir in the cheese.
4 Combine with the pasta and broccoli.

pasta with chickpeas and spinach

This is a great way of including spinach in your children's diet. It's rich in iron, folate and vitamin C.

Full of **iron** *and* **vitamins**

MAKES 4 SERVINGS

- 1 tin (410 g) chickpeas, drained and rinsed
- ½ jar (½ × 440 g) pasta sauce
- 225 g (8 oz) penne pasta
- 125 g (4 oz) baby spinach leaves
- Salt and freshly ground black pepper
- 30 g (1 oz) Parmesan cheese, grated
- 4 tbsp (60 ml) water

1 Place the chickpeas in a medium pan with the pasta, sauce together with the water. Bring gently to the boil then turn off the heat and cover.
2 Meanwhile cook the pasta in boiling water according to the directions on the packet. Drain. Stir in the spinach and allow it to wilt.
3 Spoon the pasta into a serving dish and pour the hot pasta sauce and chickpea mixture over the top. Combine together and season with salt and pepper. Top each serving with grated Parmesan.

veggie lasagne

This dish is a firm favourite with my children. The combination of pasta, vegetables, red kidney beans and cheese makes it a near-perfect balanced meal.

MAKES 4 SERVINGS

- 1 tbsp (15 ml) olive oil
- 1 onion, chopped
- 1 red pepper, chopped
- 60 g (2 oz) mushrooms, chopped
- 1 courgette, sliced
- 1 tsp (5 ml) dried basil
- Salt and freshly ground black pepper
- 1 tin (400g) red kidney beans, drained
- 400 g (14 oz) passata (smooth sieved tomatoes)
- 85 g (3 oz) mature Cheddar cheese, grated
- 9 sheets lasagne (no need to pre-cook variety)

1 Pre-heat the oven to 180 °C/350 °F/Gas mark 4.
2 Heat the oil in a large frying pan. Cook the onion for 3–4 minutes. Add the other vegetables and continue cooking for 2–3 minutes.
3 Add the basil, salt, pepper, red kidney beans and passata. Simmer for 5 minutes until the sauce thickens slightly.
4 Lay a layer of lasagne at the bottom of an oiled baking dish. Cover with one third of the bean mixture. Continue with the layers, finishing with the bean mixture.
5 Sprinkle over the Cheddar and bake for 30 minutes until bubbling and golden.

crispy vegetable gratin

This recipe is a super way of serving vegetables to children who don't like them plain.

MAKES 4 SERVINGS

- 225 g (8 oz) cauliflower, cut into florets
- 225 g (8 oz) broccoli, cut into florets
- 30 g (1 oz) butter or margarine
- 300 ml (½ pint) milk (full-fat or semi-skimmed)
- 1 tbsp (15 ml) cornflour
- 1 tsp (5 ml) Dijon mustard
- 85 g (3 oz) mature Cheddar cheese, grated
- 2 tbsp (30 ml) flaked almonds or sesame seeds

1 Cook the cauliflower and broccoli in a little fast-boiling water for 5 minutes. Drain and reserve the liquid.
2 Melt the butter in a saucepan.
3 Blend the cornflour with a little of the milk. Gradually add the remaining milk. Add to the melted butter, stirring constantly over a low heat, until the sauce thickens. Mix in the mustard and half of the cheese.
4 Arrange the vegetables in a baking dish and pour over the sauce. Sprinkle with the remaining cheese and almonds or sesame seeds.

Packed with **calcium** *and* **vitamins**

5 Place under a hot grill until golden brown.

burritos filled with beans

These tasty burritos are a new spin on pancakes, always popular with children. The bean filling is high in protein, fibre and iron.

MAKES 4 BURRITOS

Great source of **fibre** *and* **iron**

- 1 tbsp (15 ml) olive oil
- 1 onion, chopped
- 1 clove of garlic, crushed
- 1 tbsp (15 ml) taco seasoning mix (according to taste)
- 1 tin (420 g) pinto or red kidney beans (or use 175 g/ 6 oz dried beans, soaked, cooked and drained)
- 200 g (½ 400 g tin) chopped tomatoes or 200 g (7 oz) salsa
- 4 small soft wheat tortillas
- 225 g (8 oz) passata with herbs or garlic
- 60 g (2 oz) mature Cheddar cheese, grated

1 Pre-heat the oven to 180 °C/350 °F/Gas mark 4.
2 Heat the oil in a large frying pan. Sauté the onion and garlic for 5 minutes.
3 Add the taco seasoning mix, kidney beans and chopped tomatoes or salsa to the pan. Roughly mash the beans and cook for a further 3 minutes until the sauce has thickened a little.
4 Spread one quarter of the mixture over each tortilla. Roll up and place seam-side down in an oiled baking dish.
5 Spoon the passata over the tortillas; sprinkle over the cheese.
6 Cover with foil and bake for 20–30 minutes until golden.

chickpea and veggie hotpot

This one-pot dish is quick and easy to prepare and makes a perfect midweek supper. Chickpeas are rich in protein, iron and zinc. Use any variety of tinned beans in place of the chickpeas if you wish.

MAKES 4 SERVINGS

Full of **fibre** *and* **minerals**

- 1 tbsp (15 ml) olive oil
- 1 onion, chopped
- 1 garlic clove, crushed
- 2 courgettes, sliced
- 1 tsp (5 ml) dried mixed herbs
- 1 tin (400g) chopped tomatoes
- 1 tin (420 g) chick peas, drained
- 1 vegetable stock cube
- 40 g (1½ oz) Cheddar cheese, grated

1 Heat the oil in a large pan and sauté the onion and garlic for 3–4 minutes until softened. Add the courgettes and cook for a further 2 minutes.
2 Add the herbs, tomatoes, chickpeas and crumbled stock cube. Stir well and bring to the boil. Simmer for further 10 minutes, adding a little water if necessary.
3 Spoon in to a baking dish, sprinkle with grated cheese.
4 Melt the cheese under a hot grill until the cheese is bubbling.

mild spiced red lentils

Red lentils are a superb source of protein, iron, fibre and B vitamins. This mildly spiced dahl will appeal to children.

MAKES 4 SERVINGS

Packed with **protein** *and* **B vitamins**

- 1 tbsp (15 ml) sunflower oil
- 1 onion, chopped
- 1 garlic clove, crushed
- ½ tsp (2.5 ml) ground cumin
- 1 tsp (5 ml) ground coriander
- ½ tsp (2.5 ml) turmeric
- 175 g (6oz) red lentils
- 850 ml (1½ pints) water
- Salt and freshly ground black pepper

1 Heat the oil in a large pan and fry the onion for about 5 minutes. Add the garlic and spices and fry for a further 2 minutes.
2 Add the lentils and water and bring to the boil. Cover and simmer for about 30 minutes.
3 Season with salt and pepper to taste.

butter bean and leeks

This nutritious combination of pulses and vegetables is easy to prepare. You can add other vegetables, such as mushrooms or peppers, to make it a more substantial dish.

MAKES 4 SERVINGS

Rich in **fibre** *and* **vitamins**

- 1 tbsp (15 ml) olive oil
- 2 leeks, sliced
- 1 tin (400g) chopped tomatoes
- 1 tin (420g) butter beans, drained
- 150 ml (¼ pint) vegetable stock*

*Alternatively, use ½ tsp (2.5 ml) Swiss vegetable bouillon powder or ¼ vegetable stock cube dissolved in 150 ml (¼ pint) water

1 Sauté the leeks in the olive oil for about 5 minutes until the leeks are almost soft.
2 Add the remaining ingredients, stir and bring to the boil. Simmer for a further 10–15 minutes or until the sauce has thickened.

vegetable korma

Traditional kormas are made with cream. This recipe uses cashew nuts and milk in place of the cream and is a delicious way of introducing children to new flavours. Vary the vegetables according to what you have in your cupboards.

MAKES 4 SERVINGS

- 150 ml (¼ pint) milk
- 40 g (1½ oz) cashew nut pieces
- 1 tbsp (15 ml) sunflower oil
- 1 onion, sliced
- ½ tsp (2.5 ml) of each: ground cumin, garam masala and turmeric
- (Alternatively use 2 tsp/10 ml mild curry powder)
- 1 garlic clove, crushed
- 125 g (4 oz) cauliflower florets
- 1 courgette, sliced
- 60 g (2 oz) mushrooms
- 85 g (3 oz) baby corn cobs
- Salt to taste

Great source of **vitamin E** *and* **monounsaturated** *fats*

1 Bring the milk to the boil, remove from the heat and add the cashews. Leave to soak for 15 minutes, then purée until smooth using a hand blender or food processor.

2 Heat the oil in a large pan and sauté the onion for 5 minutes.

3 Add the spices and the garlic and continue cooking for 2 minutes.

4 Add the vegetables, cover and simmer for 10 minutes or until the vegetables are just tender. Season with the salt.

5 Stir in the cashew 'cream' and simmer for a further 2 minutes.

vegetable rice feast

This glorious medley of vegetables and rice is a great way of adding vegetables to children's diets. The peas and pine nuts add protein to the dish.

Full of **vitamin C** *and* **fibre**

MAKES 4 SERVINGS

- 1 tbsp (15 ml) olive oil
- 1 onion, chopped
- 1 garlic clove, crushed
- 2 celery sticks, chopped
- 1 red or yellow pepper, chopped
- 175 g (6 oz) rice (adjust the quantity according to children's appetite)
- 450 ml (¾ pint) vegetable stock*
- 125 g (4 oz) frozen peas
- Salt and freshly ground black pepper to taste
- 30 g (1 oz) pine nuts

* Alternatively, use 1½ tsp (7.5 ml) Swiss vegetable bouillon, or 1 stock cube dissolved in 450 ml (¾ pint) water

1 Heat the oil in a large pan and sauté the onion, garlic, celery and pepper for 5 minutes.
2 Add the rice and stir for another 2–3 minutes.
3 Add the stock, bring to the boil, then simmer for 15–20 minutes until the liquid has been absorbed.
4 Add the peas during the last 3 minutes of cooking, season to taste and heat through for a few more minutes. Serve sprinkled with the pine nuts.

mighty root mash

The swede and parsnips give a subtle sweetness, which children will love. They also add extra vitamins to the dish. Extra milk is used in place of the traditional butter.

Packed with **fibre** *and* **calcium**

MAKES 4 SERVINGS

- 450 g (1 lb) potatoes, peeled and cubed
- 125 g (4 oz) swede, peeled and cubed
- 1 parsnip, peeled and cubed
- 200 ml (7 fl oz) milk
- Salt and freshly ground black pepper

1 Cook the potato, swede and parsnip in a little fast-boiling water for 15–20 minutes, until tender. Drain.
2 Mash the root vegetables with the milk and seasoning. Add a little extra milk for a softer consistency.

oven potato wedges

These are a real treat for my children. These oven-baked wedges are healthier than chips as they are lower in fat and, with the skins left on, retain much of their vitamin C.

MAKES 4 SERVINGS

Good source of **fibre**

- 4 medium potatoes, scrubbed (adjust the quantity according to your children's appetite)
- 4 tsp (20 ml) sunflower
- or olive oil
- Optional: garlic powder; Parmesan cheese; chilli powder

1 Pre-heat the oven to 200 °C/400 °F/Gas mark 6.
2 Cut each potato lengthways, then cut each half into 6 wedges.
3 Place in a baking tin and turn in the oil until each piece is lightly coated.
4 Bake for 35–40 minutes turning occasionally until the potatoes are soft inside and golden brown on the outside.
5 Sprinkle on one of the optional ingredients 5 minutes before the end of cooking.

potato tacos

These tacos are easy to whip up and very nutritious, too. The beans supply protein, iron, B vitamins and fibre and make a tasty partner to the jacket potatoes.

MAKES 4 SERVINGS

- 4 potatoes
- ½ a 420 g tin refried beans, pinto beans or red kidney beans (roughly mashed)
- 4 tbsp (30 ml) mild taco sauce
- 125 g (4 oz) Cheddar cheese, grated
- 4 tbsp (60 ml) plain low-fat yoghurt
- Shredded iceberg lettuce
- 1 tomato, finely chopped

Packed with **protein** *and* **iron**

1 Pre-heat the oven to 200 °C/400 °F/Gas mark 6.
2 Scrub the potatoes and prick with a fork. Smear with a little oil and salt – this gives a crispy jacket. Bake for about 1 hour.
3 Split the cooked potato and puff it up. Heat the mashed beans. Spoon on the beans and sauce. Top with the grated cheese and yoghurt. Scatter over the lettuce and tomato.

couscous with nuts and vegetables

Couscous is easy to prepare and children enjoy its soft texture. Mix it with vegetables and nuts and it makes a delicious balanced meal.

MAKES 4 SERVINGS

- 175 g (6 oz) couscous
- 450 ml (¾ pint) vegetable stock*
- 1 tbsp (15 ml) olive oil
- 1 onion, chopped
- 1 red pepper, chopped
- 85 g (3 oz) baby corn cobs
- 1 carrot, diced
- 60 g (2 oz) dates, chopped (optional)
- 60 g (2 oz) flaked toasted almonds

*Packed with **fibre**, **vitamins** and healthy **monounsaturated** fats*

*Alternatively, use 1½ tsp (7.5 ml) Swiss vegetable bouillon or 1 stock cube dissolved in 450 ml (¾ pint) water

1 Bring the stock to the boil then remove from the heat. Pour over the couscous and leave to stand for 15 minutes until all the liquid has been absorbed.
2 Meanwhile heat the oil in a pan and sauté the onion for 5 minutes. Add the vegetables and continue cooking for about 7–10 minutes or until the vegetables are tender-crisp (not soft).
3 Fluff the couscous with a fork and stir in the vegetables, almonds and dates, if using.

potato and cheese pie

This simple dish of potatoes and cheese is, in fact, a childhood favourite of mine. My children are equally fond of it. Layer sliced leeks or broccoli florets with the cheese to increase the vegetable content.

MAKES 4 SERVINGS

- 450 g (1 lb) potatoes
- 300 ml (½ pint) milk
- 60 g (2oz) grated cheese
- 1 onion, thinly sliced
- 2 large tomatoes, sliced
- 2 eggs
- Salt and freshly ground black pepper

*Good source of complex **carbohydrates**, **antioxidants** and **calcium***

1 Pre-heat the oven to 200 °C/400 °F/Gas mark 6.
2 Peel and thinly slice the potatoes. Arrange layers of potato, cheese, onion and tomatoes in a shallow baking dish, finishing with cheese.
3 Beat the eggs with the milk, season with salt and pepper then pour over the potatoes.
4 Cover with foil and bake for 45–60 minutes until the potatoes are tender and the top golden brown.

potato soup

This is an ideal main meal soup as it is rich in energy-giving carbohydrate and the milk also provides protein and calcium. Sweet potatoes provide beta-carotene and omega-3 fatty acids, essential for brain development.

Full of **omega-3 fatty acids** *and* **beta-carotene**

MAKES 4 SERVINGS

- 2 tbsp (30 ml) olive oil
- 1 onion, chopped
- 3 medium potatoes, scrubbed and chopped into chunks
- 1 sweet potato, peeled and chopped into chunks
- 2 tsp (10 ml) Swiss vegetable bouillon powder*
- 450 ml (¾ pint) water
- 600 ml (1 pint) skimmed milk
- Freshly ground black pepper
- Handful of chopped fresh parsley or thyme if available

* Alternatively, use 1 vegetable stock cube

1 *Heat the oil in a large heavy-bottomed saucepan. Cook the onion on a low heat for 5 minutes until it becomes transparent.*
2 *Add the potatoes, stir and cook on a low heat for 2 minutes.*
3 *Add the vegetable bouillon powder and the water. Bring to the boil and simmer for about 20 minutes until the potatoes are soft.*
4 *Remove from the heat and mash or liquidise with the milk.*
5 *Return to the saucepan, add some freshly ground black pepper and fresh herbs. Heat through until just hot.*

real tomato soup

Tomato soup is a firm favourite with children. It's also a great way of hiding extra vegetables, such as carrots and red peppers. This soup is packed with vitamin C, beta-carotene and the powerful antioxidant lycopene.

Bursting with **antioxidants**

MAKES 4 SERVINGS

- 2 tbsp (30 ml) olive oil
- 1 onion, chopped
- 1 large carrot, grated
- 1 red pepper, chopped
- 1 large potato, peeled and cubed
- 2 garlic cloves, crushed
- 2 tsp (10 ml) Swiss vegetable bouillon powder*
- 1 tin (400 g) chopped tomatoes
- 750 ml (1¼ pints) water
- 1 tsp (5 ml) sugar
- Freshly ground black pepper

* Alternatively, use 1 vegetable stock cube

1 *Sauté the onion in the oil for 2–3 minutes in a large saucepan. Add the carrot, red pepper, potato and garlic and cook for a further 5 minutes.*
2 *Add the vegetable bouillon powder, tomatoes, water and sugar. Simmer for about 20 minutes or until the vegetables are soft.*
3 *Liquidise the soup using a hand blender or food processor and season with the black pepper.*

broccoli and cheese soup

This simple soup makes a nutritionally complete meal and is an ingenious way to get children to eat broccoli. It is rich in protein, fibre, vitamin C and complex carbohydrate.

MAKES 4 SERVINGS

Rich in **antioxidants** *and* **calcium**

- 1 onion, chopped
- 300 g (10 oz) broccoli florets
- 450 ml (¾ pint) vegetable stock*
- 450 ml (¾ pint) semi-skimmed milk
- 60 g (2 oz) mature Cheddar cheese, grated
- Pinch of freshly grated nutmeg (optional)
- Salt and freshly ground black pepper

*Alternatively, use 1½ tsp (7.5 ml) Swiss vegetable bouillon powder or 1 vegetable stock cube dissolved in 450 ml (¾ pint) water

1 Place the onion, broccoli and vegetable stock in a saucepan. Bring to the boil and simmer for about 15 minutes or until the vegetables are soft.
2 Liquidise the soup using a hand blender or food processor.
3 Return to the saucepan with the milk. Heat until almost at boiling point.
4 Add the grated Cheddar cheese, stirring until it melts.

butternut squash soup

This is my daughter's favourite soup. Butternut makes a wonderful soup. Its subtle sweetness appeals to children. You can substitute pumpkin or other varieties of squash for the butternut squash if you wish.

MAKES 4 SERVINGS

Bursting with **beta-carotene**

- 2 tbsp (30 ml) olive oil
- 1 onion, chopped
- 450 g (1 lb) butternut squash, peeled and chopped
- 1 large carrot, sliced
- 1 medium potato, peeled and chopped
- 2 tsp (10 ml) Swiss vegetable bouillon powder*
- 900 ml (1½ pints) water
- 1 tsp (5 ml) grated fresh ginger (or ½ tsp (2.5 ml) ground ginger)
- Freshly ground black pepper

*Alternatively, use 1 vegetable stock cube

1 Sauté the onion in the olive oil for about 5 minutes until transparent.
2 Add the butternut squash, carrot and potato and cook for a further 2–3 minutes.
3 Add the vegetable bouillon powder and water and bring to the boil. Turn down the heat and simmer for 20 minutes or until the vegetables are tender.
4 Remove from the heat. Liquidise the soup using a hand blender or food processor.
5 Season with pepper.

carrot soup

This soup is inexpensive and simple to make, and packed with beta-carotene, which boosts immunity and helps protect the body from cancer and heart disease.

MAKES 4 SERVINGS

Rich in **vitamins**

- 2 tbsp (30 ml) olive oil
- 1 onion, chopped
- 1 clove of garlic, crushed
- 675 g (1½ lb) carrots, sliced
- 900 ml (1½ pints) vegetable stock*
- Salt and freshly ground black pepper
- 1–2 tbsp (15–30 ml) fresh coriander, chopped (optional)

*Alternatively, use 3 tsp (15 ml) Swiss vegetable bouillon or 1½ vegetable stock cubes in 900 ml (1½ pints) water

1 *Sauté the onion and garlic in the olive oil for 5 minutes in a large saucepan.*
2 *Add the carrots and continue cooking for a further 2 minutes.*
3 *Add the stock and bring to the boil, then reduce the heat and simmer for 15 minutes or until the carrots are tender.*
4 *Season with the salt and pepper and add the fresh coriander.*
5 *Liquidise using a hand blender or food processor.*

vegetable soup with pasta

This soup is ideal for disguising vegetables your children may not normally choose to eat on their own. Vary the vegetables according to what you have available.

MAKES 4–6 SERVINGS

Full of **vitamins**, **minerals** *and* **fibre**

- 2 tbsp (30 ml) olive oil
- 1 onion, chopped
- 1 garlic clove, crushed
- 1 red pepper, chopped
- 1 litre (1¾ pints) vegetable stock*
- 1 tin (400 g) chopped tomatoes
- 2 large carrots, chopped
- 125 g (4 oz) cauliflower
- 2 medium potatoes, peeled and cubed
- 85 g (3 oz) small pasta shapes
- 125 g (4 oz) frozen peas
- Salt and freshly ground black pepper

*Alternatively, use 3 tsp (15 ml) Swiss bouillon or 2 vegetable stock cubes plus 1 litre (1¾ pints) water

1 *Sauté the onion, garlic and red pepper in the olive oil for 5 minutes.*
2 *Add the other vegetables, except the peas, and cook for a further 2 minutes. Add the vegetable stock, bring to the boil and simmer for about 20 minutes.*
3 *Add the pasta shapes and frozen peas about 10 minutes before the end of the cooking time. Serve. Alternatively, for a chunky thick soup, liquidise half the soup after step 2 and return to the pan.*

potato salad

This makes an excellent portable snack or lunch.
New potatoes contain twice as much vitamin C as old
potatoes. You can add extra vegetables such as
spring onions and radishes.

MAKES 4 SERVINGS

- 450 g (1 lb) new or old potatoes, cut into small chunks
  (no need to peel)
- 1 tbsp (15 ml) each of fresh chopped
  mint and parsley
- 15 cm (6 in) piece cucumber, diced
- 1 tbsp (15 ml) plain yoghurt
- 1 tbsp (15 ml) salad cream (or mayonnaise)
- Freshly ground black pepper

Good source of **vitamin C**

1 Boil the potatoes in a little fast-boiling water for 5–7
  minutes until just tender. Drain.
2 Combine the remaining ingredients together. Toss in
  the cooled potatoes and optional ingredients.

bean and tuna salad

MAKES 4 SERVINGS

- 1 tin (420 g) cannelini or butter beans, drained
- 2 tomatoes, cubed
- 1 tin (100 g) tuna in brine, drained and flaked
- 125 g (4 oz) green beans, cooked and cooled
- 1 tbsp (15 ml) red wine vinegar
- 2 tbsp (30 ml) olive oil
- Handful of fresh herbs: chives, parsley

1 Combine the tinned beans, tomatoes,
  tuna and green beans in a bowl.
2 Mix together the vinegar, oil and
  herbs and combine with the salad.

Rich in **protein**,
B vitamins, **iron**
and **fibre**.

rice salad with sweetcorn

This salad is easy to prepare and the peppers are a great source of vitamin C. The almonds provide protein and calcium.

MAKES 4 SERVINGS

- 175 g (6 oz) rice (adjust the quantity according to your children's appetite)
- 2 red peppers, chopped
- 125 g (4 oz) sultanas
- 60 g (2 oz) split almonds, roughly chopped
- 1 tin (225 g (8 oz)) sweetcorn, drained

Full of **healthy fats**, **vitamins** *and* **calcium**

1 *Cook the rice according to directions on the packet. Drain if necessary, rinse in cold water and drain again.*
2 *Place the cooled rice in a large bowl and combine with the remaining ingredients.*

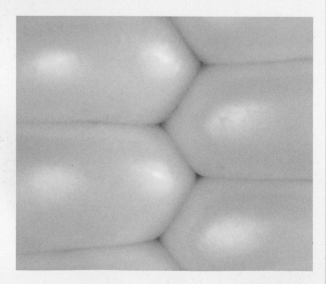

crunchy coleslaw

Children love the crunchiness of shredded cabbage combined with the smooth creaminess of mayonnaise. Raw cabbage is packed with vitamin C and, though mayonnaise is high in fat, it's mostly the healthy unsaturated kind. Add any of the optional ingredients listed below to the basic recipe – it's a great way of getting your children to eat extra raw vegetables.

MAKES 4 SERVINGS

- 125 ml (4 fl oz) low-fat mayonnaise
- 1 small head of white or green cabbage, finely shredded
- 1 large carrot, peeled and grated
- Salt and freshly ground black pepper, to taste

1 *Place the cabbage and carrots in a large bowl and stir in just enough mayonnaise to moisten the vegetables. Season with salt and pepper.*
2 *Add any of the following:*
   - *Chopped fresh parsley or chives*
   - *Pineapple chunks*
   - *Finely chopped onions or spring onions*
   - *Finely chopped peppers*
   - *Red cabbage*
   - *Broccoli*
   - *Cauliflower*
   - *Raisins*
   - *Cashews*
   - *Beetroot*
   - *Sunflower seeds*
   - *Toasted pumpkin seeds*
   - *Grated eating apple*
   - *Celery*
   - *Chicory*
   - *Celeriac*

Packed with **fibre** *and* **vitamins**

salad dressings

Most children reach for salad cream when confronted with raw salads. However, most shop-bought salad dressings are high in salt and contain artificial additives. Here are some quick and healthy alternatives that require no or very little preparation.

- A drizzle of balsamic vinegar
- A squeeze of lemon juice
- Plain yoghurt mixed with an equal quantity of salad cream
- Greek yoghurt mixed with a squeeze of lemon juice and chopped fresh parsley

olive oil and vinegar dressing

- 3 tbsp (45 ml) olive oil
- 1 tbsp (15 ml) white wine vinegar or lemon juice
- Pinch of sugar
- Pinch of salt
- Freshly ground black pepper to taste

1 *Shake the ingredients together in a screw-top jar.*

Serving Suggestion: As a dressing for leafy salads, cucumber salad and bean salads.

herb dressing

- 60 ml (2 fl oz) cider vinegar
- 2 tbsp (30 ml) orange juice
- 1 tbsp (15 ml) olive oil
- 1 garlic clove, crushed
- 1 tbsp (15 ml) chopped fresh parsley or oregano

1 *Place the ingredients in a screw-top jar and shake well to combine.*

Serving Suggestion: As a dressing for lettuce and other leaf salads, coleslaw or with cooked green vegetables such as broccoli and green beans.

tomato salsa

Tomato salsa makes a great accompaniment to tacos, grilled chicken, and meat or vegetarian burgers. It also enlivens steamed or roasted vegetables, scrambled eggs and cheese on toast.

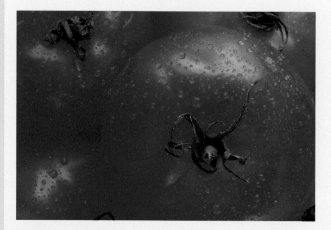

MAKES 4 SERVINGS

- 2 large ripe tomatoes or 4 ripe plum tomatoes, deseeded and finely diced
- 1–2 tbsp (15–30 ml) chopped fresh parsley or coriander
- 1 tsp (5 ml) finely chopped fresh chilli or ½ tsp (2.5 ml) dried chilli flakes (or according to your children's taste)
- 1 small clove of garlic, crushed
- 1 tbsp (15 ml) olive oil
- 2 spring onions, finely chopped
- 2 tbsp (30 ml) lemon or lime juice

1 *Combine all the ingredients in a bowl.*
2 *If time permits, chill in the fridge for about an hour before serving.*

pancakes

Pancakes are easy to make and your children will have tremendous fun tossing them! This recipe uses a half and half mixture of wholemeal and white flour to boost the vitamin, iron and fibre content. The eggs and milk are good sources of protein and the fruit fillings will provide extra vitamins.

MAKES 10–12 PANCAKES

Full of **protein** *and* **fibre**

- 70 g (2 ½ oz) plain white flour
- 70 g (2 ½ oz) plain wholemeal flour
- 2 size 3 eggs
- 250 ml (8 fl oz) milk (full-fat or semi-skimmed)
- A little vegetable oil or oil spray for frying

1 *Place all of the pancake ingredients in a liquidiser or food processor and blend until smooth.*
2 *Alternatively, mix the flours in a bowl. Make a well in the centre. Beat the egg and milk and gradually add to the flour, beating to make a smooth batter.*
3 *Place a non-stick frying pan over a high heat. Spray with oil spray or add a few drops of oil.*
4 *Pour in enough batter to coat the pan thinly and cook for 1–2 minutes until golden brown on the underside.*
5 *Turn the pancake and cook the other side for 30–60 seconds.*
6 *Turn out on a plate, cover and keep warm while you make the other pancakes.*
7 *Serve with any of the fillings below.*

Pancake fillings:
- lemon juice and sugar
- sliced banana mixed with a little honey
- sliced strawberries mixed with strawberry fromage frais
- apple purée and sultanas
- raspberries, lightly mashed with a little sugar
- frozen summer fruit mixture (thawed)
- sliced mango
- tinned pineapple
- sliced fresh or tinned apricots mixed with a little apricot yoghurt
- mixed berry fruits
- tinned cherries mixed with a little greek yoghurt
- sliced fresh nectarines or peaches

best apple crumble

This is a delicious way of adding extra fruit to your children's diet. The wholemeal flour provides extra iron, fibre and B vitamins. You can make fruit crumbles with tinned fruit and frozen fruit.

MAKES 4 SERVINGS

Filling
- 700 g (1½ lb) cooking apples, peeled and sliced
- 60 g (2 oz) raisins
- 40 g (1½ oz) sugar
- ½ tsp (2.5 ml) cinnamon
- 4 tbsp (60 ml) water

Topping
- 60 g (2 oz) plain flour
- 60 g (2 oz) wholemeal flour
- 60 g (2 oz) butter or margarine
- 40 g (1½ oz) brown sugar

Full of **vitamins** *and* **fibre**

1 *Pre-heat the oven to 190 °C/375 °F/Gas mark 5.*
2 *Place the apples, raisins, sugar and cinnamon in a deep baking dish. Combine well and pour the water over.*
3 *For the topping, put the flour in a bowl and rub in the butter until the mixture resembles coarse breadcrumbs. Mix in the sugar.*
4 *Sprinkle over the apples. Bake for 20–25 minutes.*

Variations

Substitute 700 g (1½ lb) prepared fruit for the apples. Try the following:
- apples and blackberries
- chopped rhubarb and sugar
- fresh or tinned apricots
- pears and raspberries
- fresh plums
- frozen fruits of the forest (blackberries, blackcurrants and strawberries)
- pears and bananas

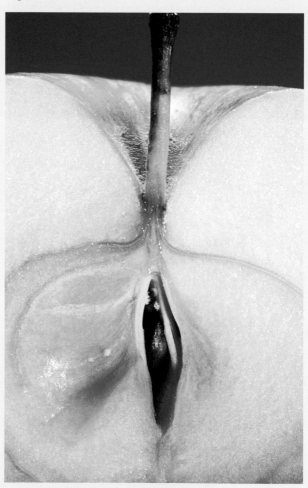

baked rice pudding

This is a great-tasting nutritious pudding, simple to make and far superior to the tinned variety. Top with fresh fruit or fruit purée.

MAKES 4 SERVINGS

- 3 tbsp (45 ml) pudding rice
- 600 ml (1 pint) milk (full-fat or semi-skimmed)
- 40 g (1½ oz) sugar
- Grated nutmeg

rich in **calcium** *and* **protein**

1 *Pre-heat the oven to 150 °C/300 °F/Gas mark 2.*
2 *Put the rice, milk and sugar in a 1.8 l (3 pint) pie dish. Stir the mixture, then grate over the nutmeg.*
3 *Bake for 1½ hours or until the milk has been absorbed and there is a light brown skin on top of the pudding.*
4 *Serve with any of the following:*
   - *ready-made fruit compote*
   - *stewed apples*
   - *sliced peaches or nectarines*
   - *stewed plums*
   - *fresh raspberries, blueberries or blackberries*

banana bread pudding

This pudding is warming and comforting, great for cold days! You can substitute raisins or stewed plums for the bananas – delicious!

MAKES 4 SERVINGS

- 6 large slices wholemeal bread
- 40 g (1½ oz) butter
- 2 small bananas, sliced
- 40 g (1½ oz) sugar
- 2 size 3 eggs
- 400 ml (14 fl oz) milk (full-fat or semi-skimmed)
- Ground cinnamon

Good source of **fibre**, **protein** *and* **calcium**

1 *Pre-heat the oven to 180 °C/350 °F/Gas mark 4.*
2 *Trim the crusts from the bread, spread lightly with butter and cut into quarters diagonally.*
3 *Arrange one third of the bread triangles in a lightly oiled baking dish.*
4 *Arrange one of the sliced bananas on top and repeat the layers, finishing with the bread.*
5 *Combine the sugar, eggs, and milk. Pour over the bread then sprinkle with cinnamon.*
6 *If you have time, allow to stand for 30 minutes. Bake for 40 minutes until the pudding is set and golden brown.*

baked bananas with chocolate buttons

This is easy enough for children to make themselves. Bananas are low in fat and rich in potassium and magnesium.

- 4 bananas
- Chocolate buttons

bursting with **minerals**

1 *Pre-heat the oven to 200 °C/400 °F/Gas mark 6.*

2 *Peel the bananas. Make a slit lengthwise in each banana, not quite cutting all the way through.*

3 *Insert the chocolate buttons in the banana slits. Wrap each banana loosely in foil and place on a baking tray.*

4 *Bake in the oven for 15 minutes. Unwrap the foil parcels when cool enough and the bananas will be oozing with delicious chocolate sauce!*

yoghurt and fruit pudding

A nutritious everyday pudding that counts towards the 5 servings of fruit or vegetables recommended for children.

Good source of **calcium** *and* **vitamins**

MAKES 1 SERVING

- 1 carton (125 g or 150 g) fruit yoghurt
- 125 g (4 oz) fresh or stewed fruit, e.g. mango, strawberries, blueberries, raspberries, peaches, bananas
- 1 tbsp (15 ml) toasted flaked almonds (or hazelnuts)

1 *Spoon half of the yoghurt into a sundae glass (or small dish).*

2 *Top with half of the fruit followed by another layer of yoghurt.*

3 *Top with the remaining fruit and nuts.*

baked custard with cherries

This baked French custard is low in fat and a good source of protein. You can substitute other fresh or tinned fruit, such as apricots, prunes, plums or pears for the cherries.

MAKES 4 SERVINGS

- 60 g (2 oz) plain flour
- 60 g (2 oz) sugar
- 2 size 3 eggs
- 350 ml (12 fl oz) milk
- 1 tin (400 g) black cherries
- Pinch of grated nutmeg
- A little sunflower oil

Rich in **vitamins** *and* **calcium**

1 *Pre-heat the oven to 200 °C/400 °F/Gas mark 6. Lightly oil a shallow baking dish with sunflower oil.*
2 *Blend the flour, sugar, eggs and milk in a liquidiser.*
3 *Arrange the cherries evenly in the bottom of the baking dish.*
4 *Pour in the batter and sprinkle the top with nutmeg.*
5 *Bake for 40–45 minutes until the custard is firm.*

summer fruit salad

Try to combine fruits with contrasting colours. This helps to make it more appealing to children. Remember, all types of berries (strawberries, raspberries, blackcurrants, blackberries, blueberries) are rich in vitamin C. Orange-coloured fruit, such as cantaloupe melon, apricots and nectarines are rich in beta-carotene. And the more intensely coloured the fruit, the better the antioxidant content.

MAKES 4 SERVINGS

- 125 g (4 oz) strawberries
- 4 slices cantaloupe melon, diced
- 1 nectarine, chopped
- 200 ml (7 fl oz) unsweetened fruit juice, e.g. pineapple, orange, orange and mango

Packed with **vitamins** *and* **fibre**

1 *Combine the prepared fruit and fruit juice in a bowl.*
2 *Spoon into individual bowls and serve with fromage frais.*

hummus

Hummus makes a great snack. Serve as a dip with crudités to encourage children to eat more vegetables. It also makes a satisfying sandwich filling or jacket potato topping.

MAKES ABOUT 600 ML (1 PINT)

- 225 g (8 oz) chickpeas, soaked overnight (or 2 tins (800 g))
- 2 garlic cloves
- 2 tbsp (30 ml) olive oil
- 4 tbsp (60 ml) tahini
- Juice of 1 lemon
- Pinch of paprika
- Freshly ground black pepper

Rich in **fibre**

1 *If using dried chickpeas drain then cook in plenty of water for about 60–90 mins or according to directions on the packet. Drain, reserving the liquid. For tinned chickpeas drain and rinse, reserving the liquid.*
2 *Purée the cooked or tinned chickpeas with the remaining ingredients with enough of the cooking liquid or juice from the tin to make a creamy consistency.*
3 *Taste and add more black pepper or lemon juice if necessary.*
4 *Chill in the fridge.*

pitta crisps

These pitta crisps are a healthy and tasty alternative to ordinary crisps. You can sprinkle them with a little grated cheese half way through cooking – delicious!

MAKES ABOUT 24

- 2 pitta breads (wholemeal or white)
- A little olive oil

Low in **fat**

1 *Pre-heat the oven to 200 °C/400 °F/Gas mark 6.*
2 *Split the pitta breads through the middle and open out so that you have four halves.*
3 *Cut each piece into triangles. Arrange on a baking tray and bake in the oven for 5–7 minutes until they become crisp and golden.*

apple muffins

These healthy muffins are excellent for lunch boxes and after-school snacks. The apples boost the nutritional value of the muffins.

MAKES 12 MUFFINS

Rich in **fibre** *and* **vitamins**

- 60 ml (2 fl oz) sunflower oil
- 125 g (4 oz) soft brown sugar
- 2 size 3 eggs
- 125 ml (4 fl oz) milk (full-fat or semi-skimmed)
- 1 tsp (5 ml) vanilla extract
- 2 apples, peeled, cored and grated
- 225 g (8 oz) self-raising flour

1 *Pre-heat the oven to 190 °C/375 °F/Gas mark 5.*
2 *Combine the oil, sugar, eggs, milk and vanilla extract in a bowl.*
3 *Stir in the grated apples and flour.*
4 *Spoon the mixture into non-stick muffin tins. Bake for 15–20 minutes until golden brown.*

fruit muffins

These are perfect refuelling snacks after sport. They are made with wholemeal flour, which is rich in fibre, iron, B vitamins and raisins, a great source of antioxidants. Make sure you pop one in your children's school bag.

MAKES 12 MUFFINS

- 125 g (4 oz) white self-raising flour
- 125 g (4 oz) wholemeal self-raising flour
- Pinch of salt
- 40 g (1½ oz) soft brown sugar
- 2 tbsp (30 ml) rapeseed oil
- 1 size 3 egg
- 200 ml (7 fl oz) milk
- 85 g (3 oz) raisins or sultanas

Packed with **vitamins**, **minerals** *and* **fibre**

1 *Pre-heat the oven to 220 °C/425 °F/Gas mark 7.*
2 *Mix the flours and salt together in a bowl.*
3 *Add the sugar, oil, egg and milk. Mix well.*
4 *Stir in the dried fruit.*
5 *Spoon into non-stick muffin tins and bake for 15–20 minutes until golden brown.*

banana muffins

These more-ish banana muffins make great after-sport or after-school snacks.

MAKES 12 MUFFINS

- 2 large ripe bananas, mashed
- 85 g (3 oz) soft brown sugar
- 4 tbsp (60 ml) rapeseed oil
- 1 size 3 egg
- 125 ml (4 fl oz) milk
- 200 g (7 oz) self-raising flour
- Pinch of salt
- ½ tsp (2.5 ml) nutmeg, grated

Packed with **minerals**

1 *Pre-heat the oven to 190 °C/375 °F/Gas mark 5.*
2 *In a bowl, mix together the bananas, sugar and oil.*
3 *Beat in the egg and milk.*
4 *Fold in the flour, salt and nutmeg.*
5 *Spoon into non-stick muffin tins and bake for 15–20 minutes.*

gingerbread people

MAKES ABOUT 10

- 60 g (2 oz) butter or margarine
- 125 g (4 oz) soft dark brown sugar
- 4 tbsp (60 ml) golden syrup
- 225 g (8 oz) plain flour
- ½ tsp (2.5 ml) bicarbonate of soda
- 2 tsp (10 ml) ground ginger
- ½ tsp (2.5 ml) cinnamon
- 1 egg

1 *Pre-heat the oven to 190 °C/375 °F/Gas mark 5. Grease a baking sheet.*
2 *Melt the butter or margarine, sugar and syrup in a saucepan.*

Low in **fat**

3 *Add the remaining ingredients and combine quickly to form a soft dough. If it is too sticky, add a little extra flour.*
4 *Roll the dough out on a floured surface then use a cutter to make the gingerbread people.*
5 *Place on the baking sheet and bake for 10 minutes or until firm to the touch and golden.*
6 *Place on a wire rack to cool. If you wish, you can decorate with icing.*

banana loaf

This delicious cake is made with wholemeal flour, brown sugar and rapeseed oil, instead of the usual white flour, white sugar and butter.

MAKES 12 SLICES

- 225 g (8 oz) self-raising wholemeal flour
- 125 g (4 oz) brown sugar
- Pinch of salt
- ½ tsp (2.5 ml) each of mixed spice and cinnamon
- 2 large ripe bananas
- 175 ml (6 fl oz) orange juice
- 2 size 3 eggs
- 4 tbsp (60 ml) rapeseed oil

*Good source of **fibre** and **minerals***

1 *Pre-heat the oven to 170 °C/325 °F/Gas mark 4.*
2 *Mix together the flour, sugar, salt and spices in a bowl.*
3 *Mash the bananas with the orange juice.*
4 *Combine the mashed banana mixture, eggs and oil with the flour mixture.*
5 *Spoon into a lightly oiled 2 lb loaf tin.*
6 *Bake for about 1 hour. Check the cake is cooked by inserting a skewer or knife into the centre. It should come out clean.*

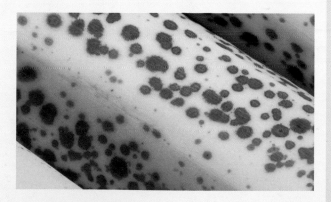

apple spice cake

This recipe is a great way of adding extra fruit to your children's diet. The grated apple and the rapeseed oil make this cake deliciously moist.

MAKES 12 SLICES

- 300 g (10 oz) self-raising flour (half wholemeal, half white)
- 125 g (4 oz) brown sugar
- 1 tsp (5 ml) cinnamon
- 2 cooking apples, peeled and grated
- 4 tbsp (60 ml) rapeseed oil
- 2 size 3 eggs
- 125 ml (4 fl oz) milk

*Good source of **vitamins** and **fibre***

1 *Pre-heat the oven to 170 °C/325 °F/Gas mark 4.*
2 *Mix together the flour, sugar and cinnamon in a bowl.*
3 *Add the grated apple, rapeseed oil, eggs and milk and combine well.*
4 *Spoon into a lightly oiled loaf tin and bake for about 1–1¼ hours. Check the cake is done by inserting a skewer or knife into the centre. It should come out clean.*

carrot cake

Traditional carrot cakes have a very high oil/fat and sugar content and are smothered in cream cheese. This version is lower in fat and sugar, and is made with grated apples and carrots.

MAKES 16 SLICES

Good source of **fibre** *and* **vitamins**

- 225 g (8 oz) self-raising flour (half wholemeal, half white)
- Pinch of salt
- 1 tsp (5ml) cinnamon
- 1 tsp (5 ml) nutmeg
- 125 g (4 oz) brown sugar
- 2 size 3 eggs
- 1 tsp (5 ml) vanilla extract
- 3 carrots, grated
- 2 apples, grated
- 4 tbsp (60 ml) rapeseed oil
- 125 ml (4 fl oz) milk

1 *Pre-heat the oven to 170 °C/325 °F/Gas mark 4.*
2 *Mix together the flour, salt, spices and sugar in a bowl.*
3 *Stir in the eggs, vanilla, carrots, apples, oil and milk.*
4 *Line a loaf tin or a 20 cm (8 in) round cake tin with greaseproof paper. Spoon in the cake mixture.*
5 *Bake for about 1 hour. Check that the cake is cooked by inserting a skewer or knife into the centre. It should come out clean.*

fruit cake

The dried fruit and grated apple add plenty of vitamins and fibre to this cake. It makes a nutritious snack anytime.

MAKES 16 SLICES

- 225 g (8 oz) self-raising flour
- 85 g (3 oz) brown sugar
- 1 tsp (5 ml) cinnamon
- 2 size 3 eggs
- 4 tbsp (60 ml) rapeseed oil
- 1 tsp (5 ml) vanilla extract
- 225 g (8 oz) dried fruit mixture
- 1 apple, grated
- 85 ml (3 fl oz) milk

Packed with **fibre**

1 *Pre-heat the oven to 170 °C/325 °F/Gas mark 4.*
2 *Mix together the flour, sugar and cinnamon in a bowl.*
3 *Make a well in the centre and add the eggs, oil, vanilla, dried fruit, apple and milk. Combine together well.*
4 *Spoon into a 20 cm (8 in) round or square baking tin and bake for about 1¼–1½ hours. Check the cake is cooked by inserting a skewer or knife into the centre. It should come out clean.*

ginger spice cake

This delicious cake is lower in fat and sugar than the traditional version, yet is deliciously moist as it is made with rapeseed oil.

MAKES 10 SLICES

- 200 g (7 oz) plain flour
- 1 tsp (5 ml) bicarbonate of soda
- 1 tsp (5 ml) cinnamon
- 1 tsp (5 ml) ginger
- 1 tsp (5 ml) ground cloves
- 1 size 3 egg
- 125 g (4 oz) soft brown sugar
- 4 tbsp (60 ml) rapeseed oil
- 200 ml (7 oz) low-fat plain yoghurt
- 1 tbsp (15 ml) Demerara sugar
- 1 tbsp (15 ml) pecan nuts, chopped

Rich in **monounsaturated** *fats*

1 Pre-heat the oven to 160 °C/325 °F/Gas mark 3.
2 Lightly oil a 1.5 l (2½ pint) loaf tin.
3 Place the flour, bicarbonate of soda and spices in a bowl and mix together.
4 Whisk the egg, sugar and oil together until light and fluffy. Stir in the low-fat yoghurt and mix well.
5 Gently fold in the flour and spice mixture.
6 Spoon into the prepared tin and sprinkle with the Demerara sugar and chopped nuts.
7 Bake for 45 minutes. Check the cake is cooked by inserting a skewer or knife into the centre. It should come out clean. Allow to cool for a few minutes before turning out on to a cooling rack.

wholemeal raisin biscuits

These biscuits are far healthier than bought ones. They are lower in sugar and higher in fibre.

MAKES 20 BISCUITS

- 225 g (8 oz) wholemeal plain flour
- 40 g (1½ oz) brown sugar
- 85 g (3 oz) raisins
- 2 tbsp (30 ml) rapeseed oil
- 1 size 3 egg
- 4 tbsp (60 ml) milk

Good source of **fibre**

1 Pre-heat the oven to 180 °C/350 °F/Gas mark 4.
2 Combine the flour, sugar and raisins in a bowl.
3 Stir in the oil, egg and milk and lightly mix together until you have a stiff dough.
4 Place spoonfuls of the mixture onto a lightly oiled baking tray.
5 Bake for 12–15 minutes until golden brown.

apricot bars

Dried apricots are packed with beta-carotene, a powerful antioxidant that's also good for the skin.

MAKES 8 BARS

- 125 g (4 oz) self-raising white flour
- 60 g (2 oz) sugar
- 125 g (4 oz) dried apricots
- 6 tbsp (90 ml) orange juice
- 2 size 3 eggs
- 125 g (4 oz) sultanas

Good source of **beta-carotene**

1 *Pre-heat the oven to 180 °C/350 °F/Gas mark 4.*
2 *Mix together the flour and sugar in a bowl.*
3 *Blend together the apricots and juice in a liquidiser or food processor until smooth.*
4 *Add the apricot purée, eggs and sultanas to the flour and sugar. Mix together.*
5 *Spoon the mixture into an 18 cm (7 in) square cake tin. Bake for 30–35 minutes until golden brown. Allow to cool. Cut into 8 bars.*

cereal bars

These highly nutritious bars are made from oats and muesli, which provide slow-release sustained energy. They are lower in fat than commercial cereal bars.

MAKES 12 BARS

Full of **fibre**

- 175 g (6 oz) oats
- 85 g (3 oz) no added sugar muesli
- 150 g (5 oz) dried fruit mixture
- 3 tbsp (45 ml) honey, clear or set
- 2 egg whites
- 175 ml (6 fl oz) apple juice

1 *Pre-heat the oven to 180 °C/350 °F/Gas mark 4.*
2 *Combine the oats, muesli and dried fruit in a bowl.*
3 *Warm the honey in a small saucepan until it is runny. Add to the bowl.*
4 *Stir in the remaining ingredients.*
5 *Press the mixture into a lightly oiled 18 × 28 cm (7 × 11 in) baking tin. Bake for 20–25 minutes until golden. When cool, cut into bars.*

banana shake

This simple, nutritious shake makes a great refuelling drink at any time of the day.

MAKES 2 SERVINGS

- 250 ml (8 fl oz) milk (full-fat or semi-skimmed)
- 2 ripe bananas, sliced
- Few ice cubes, crushed

Good source of **calcium** *and* **potassium**

1 *Put the milk, crushed ice and banana in a smoothie maker, blender or food processor. Blend until smooth, thick and bubbly.*

strawberry shake

MAKES 2 SERVINGS

- 150 ml (¼ pint) milk (full-fat or semi-skimmed)
- 1 carton (125 g) low-fat strawberry yoghurt
- 1 handful of strawberries
- Few ice cubes, crushed

1 *Put the milk, crushed ice and strawberries in a smoothie maker, blender or food processor. Blend until smooth, thick and bubbly.*

Full of **vitamin C**

banana smoothie

This velvet-thick smoothie is made simply from fruit and yoghurt, and doubles as a nourishing dessert.

MAKES 2 SERVINGS

- 1 large ripe banana
- 1 carton (150 g) plain bio-yoghurt
- 2 tsp (10 ml) honey
- 60 ml (2 fl oz) apple juice

Rich in **potassium** *and* **magnesium**

1 *Blend all the ingredients in a smoothie maker, blender or food processor, then serve.*

mango and strawberry smoothie

Mangoes are a terrific source of beta-carotene, while strawberries provide lots of vitamin C. A super nutritious drink!

MAKES 2 SERVINGS

Packed with **vitamins**

- 1 small mango
- 125 g (4 oz) strawberries
- 1 banana
- 200 ml (7 fl oz) apple juice

1 *Peel the banana and peel and stone the mango. Place all the fruit in smoothie maker, blender or food processor and blend until smooth.*

2 *Add the apple juice and blend for a few more seconds. If you wish, you can reduce the quantity of juice to give a thicker drink.*

berry smoothie

This drink is bursting with vitamin C and cancer-protective phytochemicals.

Rich in **antioxidants**

MAKES 2 SERVINGS

- 225 g (8 oz) mixture of fresh or frozen berries, e.g. raspberries, blueberries, strawberries, blackcurrants
- 1 carton (150 g) raspberry bio-yoghurt
- 200 ml (7 fl oz) milk (full-fat or semi-skimmed)

1 *Put all the ingredients in smoothie maker, blender or food processor and blend until smooth.*

tropical smoothie

The mango and papaya provide lots of beta-carotene and the lime juice is rich in vitamin C.

MAKES 2 SERVINGS

- 1 mango, peeled and stoned
- 4 slices fresh or tinned pineapple
- 1 papaya, peeled and de-seeded
- Juice of 1 lime
- Ice cubes

Bursting with **vitamins**

1 *Put the fruit and ice in smoothie maker, blender or food processor and blend until smooth.*

peach and raspberry smoothie

This smoothie is a great energiser and immune booster.

MAKES 2 SERVINGS

Full of
beta-carotene,
vitamin C *and*
potassium

- 1 banana
- 1 peach
- 125 g (4 oz) raspberries (or strawberries)
- 125 ml (4 fl oz) orange juice

1 *Place all the fruit and the orange juice in a smoothie maker, blender or food processor and blend until smooth.*

strawberry and banana shake

Banana and strawberries make a delicious combination. This nutritious drink makes a great after-school or post-exercise drink.

MAKES 2 SERVINGS

Great source of
potassium,
vitamin C *and*
calcium

- 1 banana
- 125 g (4 oz) strawberries
- 1 carton (150 g) strawberry bio-yoghurt
- 120 ml (4 fl oz) milk (full-fat or semi-skimmed)

1 *Place the fruit, yoghurt and milk in smoothie maker, blender or food processor and blend until smooth.*

online resources

www.kidshealth.org

A US-based website offers expert health, nutrition and fitness advice for parents, kids and teenagers.

www.nutrition.org.uk

The website of the British Nutrition Foundation, contains information, fact sheets and educational resources on nutrition and health.

www.foodstandards.gov.uk

The website of the government's Food Standards Agency has news of nutrition surveys, nutrition and health information.

www.vegsoc.org

The Vegetarian Society's website provides information on vegetarian nutrition for children as well as general nutrition, health and recipes.

www.weightconcern.com

Excellent information on obesity issues, including a section on children's health and a BMI calculator.

www.foodcomm.org.uk

The website of the Food Commission, an independent food watchdog, contains up-to-date news of nutrition campaigns, surveys and the Parents Jury.

www.healthedtrust.com

An excellent on-line resource for news and information on health for young people with useful sections on school food and drink

www.aso.org.uk

The website of the Association for the Study of Obesity and includes the Obesity Resource Information Centre (ORIC), which has information on childhood obesity.

www.eatright.org

The website of the American Dietetic Association, gives nutrition news, tips and resources.

www.bda.uk.com

The website of the British Dietetic Association includes fact sheets and information on healthy eating for children.

www.nutrio.com

A US nutrition and fitness website, which includes a useful section on kids' nutrition and fitness.

www.edauk.com

The website of the Eating Disorders Association, offering information and help on all aspects of eating disorders.

index

recipe index